Big Money, Less Risk

Trade Options

Mark Larson

Marketplace Books
Columbia, Maryland

OTHER BOOKS BY MARK LARSON

Technical Charting for Profits

Trade Stocks Online

12 Simple Technical Indicators that Really Work Course Book and DVD

Disclaimers

1. Trading securities can involve high risk and the loss of any funds invested. Investment information provided may not be appropriate for all investors, and is provided without respect to individual investor financial sophistication, financial situation, investing time horizon, or risk tolerance.

2. Options trading is generally more complex than stock trading and may not be suitable for some investors. Granting options and some other options strategies can result in the loss of more than the original amount invested. Before trading options a person should review the document, characteristics and risks of standardized options, available from your broker or any exchange on which options are traded.

3. The securities used as examples in this book are used for illustrative purposes only. Investools, thinkorswim, and/or Mark Larson are not recommending that you buy or sell these securities. Past performance shown in examples may not be indicative of future performance. Mark Larson is not affiliated with thinkorswim, inc.

4. Rolling Along Investments nor any of its employees or associates offer any financial or tax advice and is not in the business of transacting trades. Please consult your tax attorney, licensed broker or C.P.A. in regards to any tax information or asset structuring.

Library of Congress Cataloging-in-Publication Data

Larson, Mark L., 1965-
  Big money, less risk : trade options / by Mark Larson.
      p. cm.
  Includes bibliographical references and index.
  ISBN-13: 978-1-59280-341-5 (hardcover : alk. paper)
  ISBN-10: 1-59280-341-5 (hardcover : alk. paper) 1. Stock options. 2. Options (Finance) 3. Investment analysis. I. Title.
  HG6042.L37 2008
  332.63'2283--dc22
                                 2008041418

Printed in the United States of America.

Big Money, Less Risk: Trade Options

Table of Contents

Foreword

The world of options is often daunting and confusing on many levels. First, the terminology is highly specialized with a lot of cross-over use of expressions, especially when describing strategies. Second, quantitatively evaluating risk is elusive because the possible range covers the entire spectrum when trading options.

Mark Larson has compiled a book that features a series of common sense option strategies every trader should master. He explains these in straightforward language and expands examples with graphics, definitions, and sidebars. Larson has made the mastery of a few valuable concepts easy for every investor and trader.

Anyone who has tried to read books explaining how to trade options may be discouraged by the complexity and technical jargon of this industry. But rather than giving up, traders need to go through Larson's book. The options market has grown to become a major factor in the market today, and this trend is going to continue into the future. Tomorrow's successful trader will include options as a matter of course, to enhance profits, hedge risks, and protect profits in stock and other positions. Options have been available to the public only since 1973. That year, only 1.1 million contracts were traded. In 2007, according to the Chicago Board Options Exchange (CBOE), nearly 2.9 billion contracts were traded. This includes options on stocks, indices, futures, and mutual funds. The expanse of the market itself has broadened in recent years.

Perhaps the greatest cause for this expansion has been the Internet. Today, you can trade options without a stockbroker. You can use online discount services, which enable you to complete a round-trip trade (buy and sell) for less than one-quarter of a point in trading fees. This is a vast improvement over the past. When you had to use a stockbroker to execute an options trade, it was much more expensive; and the time delay made many strategies ineffective or impractical. Making matters worse, many stockbrokers, although licensed to execute options trades, really didn't understand the market.

With Mark Larson's book, you gain a good start in the market of options, where you can leverage your capital, control the level of risk, and use a range of strategies to manage your portfolio. There is nothing new about the options concept, but for the modern American investor or trader, the application of the principles behind options make trading more flexible than ever, and potentially more profitable as well. Larson shares some insider secrets and provides valuable tips for using options effectively, picking the best and safest strategies, and coordinating option selection with a few basic technical indicators to help you better time your trades.

Don't let the options market intimidate you. Rather, look at this market as an opportunity to beat the averages, improve portfolio returns, and cut losses. There are so many ways that options can be put to work for relatively little investment that virtually every trader will benefit from Mark Larson's book.

—MICHAEL C. THOMSETT Best-selling author of *Getting Started in Options, Mastering Technical Analysis, Mastering Fundamental Analysis*, and over 40 other trading and investing titles

Preface

THE PREFACE OF A book is often the second place one goes after reading the inside cover of the book. If you're reading this section and haven't yet purchased this book, I can assure you that *Big Money, Less Risk: Trade Options* will be a book you will have a hard time putting down. It will also be a book that will teach you things about the stock market that you may not have known existed. I'm not talking about why the stock market goes up or down; I'm talking about how to make money when it goes up or down. I'm talking about investment strategies that allow you to have huge returns on your money with the use of very little money. I'm talking about how to purchase good stocks at discount prices. I'm talking about placing option type trades that allow you to be wrong and still make 10, 20, 30% return on your money in one month.

I wrote each chapter with a lot of thought, taking over 10 years of teaching and trading experience to help you learn the various types of investment strategies that the experts use to make money, such as writing covered calls, selling naked put options, and placing vertical spread trades or iron condors. This book is based on my belief that success in the stock market is determined by how much money you can make each and every month, instead of waiting to see how much you might have when you retire.

As you read, I would encourage you to keep in mind that no book will determine your wealth; it's the experience of what you've learned and the coaching/mentoring that will determine your true financial wealth. We often look for the shortest path of resistance or the most inexpensive way to learn something; I ask that you please be willing to properly educate yourself and not just take what you read for granted.

Please do not place your hard-earned money at risk until you have perfected your investment strategies of choice. As I have always said to my students, if you were to look in the dictionary for the words "education," "knowledge," "money," and "wealth" you would see that wealth comes last, and there's a good reason for that. As you make your final decision to purchase this book or other educational material, please don't look at the cost. Instead, look at the value that this knowledge will bring. I assure you that this information is priceless, and that this book will more than pay for itself.

As a matter of fact, I would ask that you purchase a second or third book for the people that are closest to you. Give them the gift of learning how to let their money work for them. Know that you're giving them an incredible opportunity to learn how to truly make money in the stock market regardless if it goes up, down, or even sideways.

I want to thank you from deep down in my heart because I will donate a percentage of each book that is sold to the Alzheimer's Foundation in honor of the thousands of lives that are lost to this disease, including my father who passed away at the young age of 63 on January 18, 2005. I'm saddened by his death in so many ways; wishing he could be here trading with me, wishing we could be fishing together, but more so wishing my son Mason could have been able to see what a great father my dad was. Unfortunately, my dad passed before Mason was able to meet him.

Soon, the day will come when I will sit down with Mason and tell him what a great father my dad was. I will also promise Mason that being able to spend time with him is my first priority because the thing I regret is that I didn't spend enough time with my father. At that time, I will encourage Mason, as I would you, to "learn how to let your money work for you" instead of always working for your money.

Remember, a wise man or wise woman is not one who measures wealth with his or her financial balance; it is one who measures his or her wealth with knowledge. Knowledge is priceless; you can take all of my money but you can't take my knowledge, which gives me the ability to create and keep my wealth. Enjoy your journey as you read each of these powerful chapters.

—MARK LARSON

Acknowledgement

I HAVE SO MUCH to be thankful for and so many to thank, but I must begin with my family because without their support I wouldn't have the freedom to write this book and help others. Having family time is the most important reason I trade the market.

I would like to thank all the people at Traders' Library for publishing my book along with the other educational programs I've produced; the family at Investools for giving me the opportunity to travel the world and teach others how to become successful investors; and the family at thinkorswim for giving me the awesome tools to trade the market. And, of course, I'd like to thank you for purchasing this book and supporting me. You, the student, are my greatest inspiration. If you continue to learn, I'll continue to teach.

Introduction

WHO AM I AND why would I write a book about the stock market? I'm a sponge for knowledge that decided in 1998 to search out the biggest known names in the stock market and learn what makes them successful. I knew nothing about the stock market when I began; yet, with a small amount of money, the right education, dedication, and inspiration, I changed my financial life beyond my greatest dreams. Today, my greatest inspiration is sharing with others how they too can increase their rate of return, reduce their risk, and create a plan of financial consistency within the stock market. My drive as a writer is to simply create the best stock market options book. Now, don't get me wrong, there are several great books out there written by the giants of this industry such as Larry McMillan and Bernie Schaffer. I consider this book as another step forward.

In this book, I'll refer to basic options as "get rich strategies" and advanced options as "stay rich strategies." I'll also cover the importance of option pricing, implied volatility (how much an option may be over-priced), the Greeks such as delta, theta, and gamma, and the probability of your option expiring profitable. I will also share with you how to properly use the Greeks and how you can use a probability calculation to determine the odds of your option trade making or losing money. Most important, I will walk you through some of my favorite indicators and show you how they will form the basis of your options trading success.

As you read, I want you to keep in mind that success at any level will not be obtained unless you have a blueprint to follow. One of the most important rules within my blueprint is "when to sell," and this is something I will teach you within these pages.

WHY DO YOU NEED THIS BOOK?

I've always believed that what goes up most come down. As I stated in my second stock market book titled *Technical Charting for Profits*: "then came April 2000 when the bull decided to quit running and appeared to give in to the bear as we began a true stock market correction, one that many investors never experienced before."

Why am I sharing this with you? Because you need to be better than buy and hold, and you need to be able to identify when to sell so you can avoid large losses. Just eight years later, in January 2008, we seem to be beginning another bear market correction or what I would even call a crash.

As I'm writing this (the first week of January 2008), the stock market has stopped moving up and is quickly heading lower into a bearish market, making it the worst January since 1932 and soon-to-be the worst January ever. This comes after the Dow Jones reached an all-time record high of 14,200 in October of 2007 before dropping 2,000 points to about 12,000, most of which occurred in the first half of January 2008. Then came January 22, 2008: the market opened down even lower as the Dow Jones dropped another 450 points prior to the open of the market, which created a drop of over 2,500 points. The S&P 500 also reached a record high in October 2007 of 1,575 before dropping over 250 points by the third week of January 2008. This took it right back to its price during mid-2006. And, since the explosion of the dot-com era, the NASDAQ hasn't been able to do much at all.

You Need to Know How to Invest During Good Times and Bad

What should this information tell you? If you're an investor, then you need to be able to take profits off the table, and, more important, you must know how to trade the downside of the market. The bear market of 2000-2003 was different then the 2008 correction. In 2000, we saw an over-inflated dot-com boom, while in 2008, we saw a crash related to the broad economy but more specifically, the housing industry and the subprime mortgages.

Housing costs skyrocketed between 2000 and 2005 because interest rates were low enough that homeowners and investors could still afford to buy. Yet, those that didn't time the housing market right could not flip the house for a profit and were quickly in danger of losing the home in a short-sale to the bank or foreclosure. This created more homes for sale than buyers while interest rates climbed higher and higher and bad sub-prime loans with 5-year balloon payments forced the Federal Reserve to step in and make an emergency rate cut of 75 base points. Did this sudden rate cut stop the problem? Not at all, many say it was just a bandage as the housing industry continued to have trouble for years to come.

An old saying states that if the month of January ended positive, then the year would end higher than where it began and visa versa. I don't know if the market will move higher or lower by year-end, but I can share with you a chart showing that the stock market was showing great signs of weakness. If you're going to hold stocks after viewing this chart (Figure I.1), then I would do so only using a small bag of money. There are sure signs to "SELL" and to limit your risk, which might even mean that your money sits in a money market account until the bull market returns.

CAUTION

The Buy and Hold Mindset
Many people mistakenly believe that if they buy a stock and hold it over a long enough period of time, then they will eventually make money on that stock. This belief stems from the fact that over the course of history, the stock market as a whole has always trended higher.

However, this reasoning is faulty. First, your particular stock does not have to trend higher and can in fact dive all the way to zero. Second, buy and hold investing is not an educated strategy: you need to be able to actively manage your money. And that means taking responsibility for it in up, down, and sideways markets. This book is a good first step in learning how to make your money work for you instead of wishing for a market miracle.

If today is January 22nd 2008 and the Dow Jones opens down over 450 points, then who is selling if you're not? The large institutions are selling. Remember, you need more sellers than buyers for the market to drop and more buyers than sellers for the market to increase. It's a business of opportunity and any time the largest investors see an opportunity to take profits and move the markets up or down, they will. In this case, it was time to take the bullish profits off the table and short the market and drive it down. If you are buying and holding, you are helpless to this movement.

Figure I.1 is a reference as to when the market showed bearish signs. You'll notice a large line—this is the 200-day moving average, which we will discuss in more detail later. When the Dow

FIGURE I.1 —————————— Dow Jones Chart

Sign of bear market

200 day Moving Average

Break of support

Dow opens 451 lower

14,500
14,250
14,000
13,750
13,500
13,250
13,000
12,750
12,500
12,250
12,000
11,750

07 Mar Apr May Jun Jul Aug Sep Oct Nov Dec 08 Feb

For color charts go to: www.traderslibrary.com/TLECorner • Chart by: thinkorswim.com

dropped below that level in December at the price of 13,250, this warned investors that the market was going to drop. And it did drop: a whole 1600 points. A second sign of weakness was seen when the stock price dropped below 12,750, which was the Dow Jones support level. When stocks drop below their support levels, this also is a sign of downward weakness. We will discuss these concepts later in the book.

If you find this type of chart (with technical indicators) to be helpful, you'll really enjoy chapter one as I outline some of the most rewarding technical indicators and how to use them to determine when to trade both the bullish (upward) and the bearish (downward) markets.

You Need to Change Your Mindset

Based on examples like this one, you'll need to make a commitment to break out of buy and hold if you want more consistent returns. If you're going to be successful, you'll need to learn new strategies like the ones in this book. Many times when you choose to sell, it's often because you're forced to do it. You need a mindset change to your financial blueprint; this will allow you to approach the market as a business opportunity for purposes of generating monthly cash flow. A great book to help you change that mind set and create a financial blueprint for success is *Secrets of the Millionaire Mind* by T. Harv Eker.

Make Your Money Work for You

Your money needs to be working for you or you'll never be able to stop working. If you're watching the stock market drop again for the second time in eight years, then you're not doing something right. This book will be of great help but please don't think that a book by itself will make you successful at trading the stock market. Its purpose is to share the many ways that professional traders trade the market. Hopefully, this will inspire you to continue your education on the markets.

Let me give you this thought before moving on: "more money is spent on a new automobile than financial education." Statistically, households paid more for their cars than they did to learn how to manage their investment accounts. So, if your investment accounts, or even better yet your retirement accounts, are larger than the cost of your car, and you paid more for your car then the education to manage your money, then you're going about it the wrong way. When you retire from your current employer/occupation, you need to know how to create enough monthly income to cover your expenses or the cost of inflation may affect your family and lifestyle.

Your ultimate goal is to have a large enough bag of money (which I call the "stay rich" bag) that, if need be, can take care of your family two generations below you. Five percent of the wealthiest people have financially planned for two generations lower, and for some of you, it may be one generation above you if your parents (or worse your grandparents) did not adequately plan.

The "Get Rich" and "Stay Rich" Money Bags

Let's talk a little about the two different bags of investment money and what each one of them represents. The first bag or the "get rich" bag consists of no more than 10% of your total stock market net worth and should only be used for high risk trades that can offer higher rates of return, such as buying either call (bullish market) or put (bearish market) options. We'll refer to these types of trades as directional trades because the stock must move in the direction of your investment or you'll lose your investment due to expiration.

Let's break the numbers down and say that if your total investment in the stock market was $100,000, then your "get rich" bag would only consist of $10,000 for the use of buying call or put options. Your rates of return would be much greater than those within your "stay rich" bag. The $10,000 bag should not affect your family's lifestyle if you were to lose the entire amount. On the other hand, the second bag of money, or the "stay rich" bag, which in this example will consist of $90,000, would affect your family's lifestyle. For this reason, you would be making more conservative trades such as purchasing stock for covered calls, or even better yet spread trades, with this bag of money.

Let me address the 10% "get rich" bag. Your rates of return will be typically much larger simply because you're using leverage. For example, if you were to spend $3,000 and purchase 5 option contracts, you could see the investment increase to $4,500 or greater; this would give you a rate of return of about 50%.

The important thing you must remember about buying call or put options is that the stock must move in your selected direction (calls up and puts down) or you will lose the entire $3,000, unless you're using a stop loss order (which I'll discuss later).

Let me give you a better example of a call option: Apple Computer was trading at $140.85 on March 24th and the purchase of a $140 call option cost $3.85 per share; so, the purchase of 5 call option contracts cost $1,925. On April 2nd the call option was trading for $12.85 per share for a profit of $9 per share ($12.85 x 500 = $6,425) and a rate of return of 234%. That's leverage at its best, when it allows a 234% return on a stock that moved up from $140.85 to $150.35. Now as for the "stay rich" bag of money, you won't see those types of returns; they will be more along the lines of 15 to 24% per trade (average of 4 week trades). This type of an investment, however, can allow for the stock to move up,

---

LINGO

Rate of Return is what you gain or lose on an investment over a specific time period. It is expressed as a percentage increase over the initial investment cost. (Source: Investopedia.com)

Rate of Return = Your total profit/Your capital x 100

In this example: $9/3.85 x 100 = 234%

---

down, or sideways and still be profitable. In other words, your "get rich" bag of money doesn't allow much room for error and your "stay rich" bag does. You may find yourself moving more to the "stay rich" bag as you get closer to retirement; this will reduce your risk and create more consistency.

The Four Quarters Of Your Working Life
Age 25 – 34 First Quarter
Age 35 – 44 Second Quarter
Age 45 – 54 Third Quarter
Age 55 – 64 Fourth Quarter

If you are near retirement, then you've worked four quarters of your life to build this bag of money; now it's time to learn how to keep what you've worked so hard for and learn how to let your money work for you. Although we often make more financial mistakes earlier in life, you must have built your net worth by the end of the fourth quarter of your working life. At this point, you must know how to have your money work for you or you will be forced to go back to work. If you build your wealth before the end of your fourth quarter and you know how to successfully trade the stock market, I'd say that you're in a better position of retiring early and staying retired.

UNDERSTANDING THE POWER OF OPTIONS FOR RETIREMENT

My goal is for you to understand the power of purchasing put options in bear markets and call options in bull markets. These tools will help you not only weather any financial storm but make consistent profits during one. This will become essential during retirement when you will be reliant on the income from your investments.

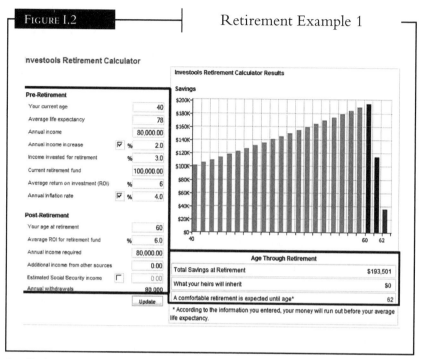

| FIGURE I.2 | Retirement Example 1 |

For color charts go to: www.traderslibrary.com/TLECorner • Chart by: investools.com

Let's go back to January 2008. I can think of only one reason for the big drop—inflation. This equals bad money management. The cost of living continues to increase year over year and 95% of the people in the world are not educated on how to plan for inflation increases. I know we can blame the President, the war, the cost of gas, the cost of medical care, the bad sub-prime real estate loans, maybe even that fact that the baby boomers began collecting Social Security early beginning on January 1, 2008. All of these are good reasons for the stock market to go down, but does it really matter why the stock market or economy isn't doing well? No; because if you have a good financial blue print, then the cost of such things as gas and health

The key to a good retired life: spend less than you make and know how much your investments are generating each month.

care shouldn't affect your family. It's a simple concept: spend less than you make.

I recently had lunch with a couple of my stock market students and asked them: "How is it that you've been able to live a good retired life?" Their answer was "spend less then you make and know how much your investments are generating each month." They are happy with an extra $2,000 to $3,000 of income each month. Would that money help you? Or is it $5,000 to $6,000 per month? This really boils down to how well you have prepared for your retirement and how well your money will be working for you.

As you read, I can only hope that you become more inspired to live the dream of financial independence, and more so, that you take the right steps to build and keep your wealth. Take a look at my financial calculator, which will give you a better idea of what you'll need to do to be financially independent when you retire. Let's break down a few different examples.

Retirement Example 1: You're Out of Money in Two Years

Beginning with Retirement Example 1 (Figure I.2), you'll notice that I selected criteria that applies to either male or female and/or both, if living together, with a household income of about $80,000 per year with a current age of 40, a life expectancy of 78, a goal to retire at the age 60, and a saving of $100,000. This gives you 20 years to build your income using a 6% rate of return, which is an average yearly rate of return. I have considered an annual income increase of 2% a year with 3% of your total income going to retirement. This example shows that you'll have about $193,501 at the age of 60, which would be an early retirement. However, with a 6% return and a needed annual income of $80,000, you'll run out of money at the age of 62.

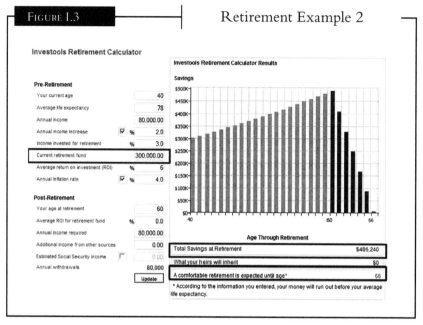

For color charts go to: www.traderslibrary.com/TLECorner • Chart by: investools.com

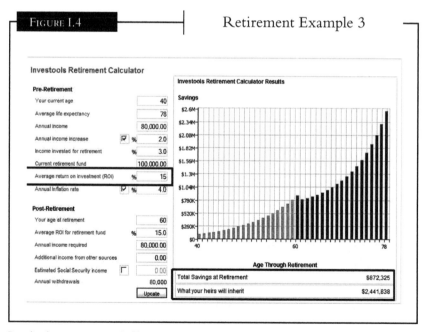

For color charts go to: www.traderslibrary.com/TLECorner • Chart by: investools.com

RETIREMENT EXAMPLE 2: YOU'RE OUT OF MONEY IN SIX YEARS

Now let's look at a second example (Figure I.3) where we have changed only one thing: the amount of money you have to invest went from $100,000 to $300,000. The results are not much different: instead of having $193,501 at the age 60, you now have $486,240 at a 6% return and yearly expenses of $80,000. Instead of running out of money at the age 62, you'll now run out of money at the age 66.

Sorry to be the bearer of bad news, but this is reality, which is why 95% of people need some type of government financial aid. The good news is that a lack of money at retirement can be solved if you change one factor to the equation, the rate of return. I know many of you may have thought that we would change the amount of money needed in your retirement fund or increase the age at

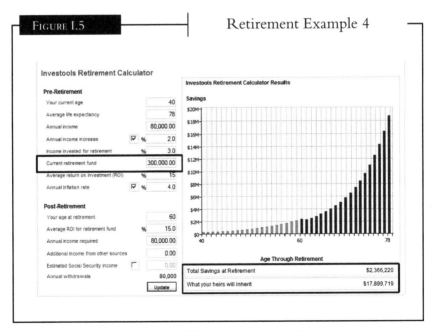

FIGURE I.5   Retirement Example 4

For color charts go to: www.traderslibrary.com/TLECorner • Chart by: investools.com

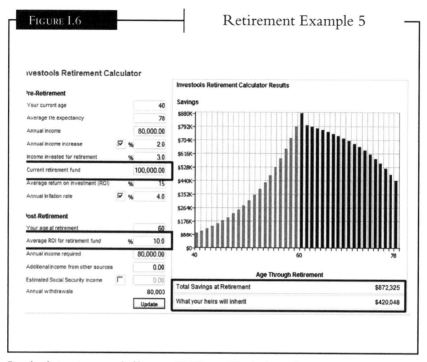

| FIGURE I.6 | Retirement Example 5 |

For color charts go to: www.traderslibrary.com/TLECorner • Chart by: investools.com

which you retire, or even reduce your lifestyle expectancy (income). You can do any of those things, but I prefer to focus on the rate of return.

RETIREMENT EXAMPLE 3: INCREASE YOUR RATE OF RETURN AND THRIVE

In Figure I.4, by increasing just the rate of return from 6% pre-retirement and 6% post-retirement to 15% pre-retirement and 15% post-retirement (leaving everything else the same), you now have $872,325 at retirement and $2,441,838 to pass onto your heirs.

For those of you that have put aside more money prior to the age of 60, Figure I.5 shows your savings at retirement being $2,366,220 with your heirs inheriting $17,899,719 [that is if your retirement

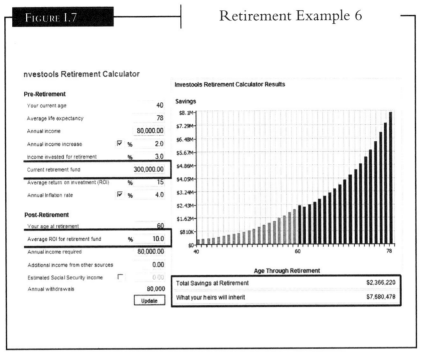

FIGURE I.7 ——————— | Retirement Example 6 ⌐

For color charts go to: www.traderslibrary.com/TLECorner • Chart by: investools.com

fund had a $300,000 balance and you received an average return of 15% both pre and post retirement].

RETIREMENT EXAMPLE 4: CHOOSE CONSERVATIVE STRATEGIES DURING RETIREMENT

Now, I think that during your retirement years you should choose investment strategies that are more conservative. Instead of a 15% return post-retirement, let's use a more conservative 10%. This should still be appealing while having less risk. In Figure I.6, we've taken the $100,000 retirement fund and dropped the post-retirement interest rate to 10%, which gives you $872,325 at retirement and $420,048 to pass on to your heirs.

With a current retirement fund of $300,000 (Figure I.7) and an average rate of return of 10% post retirement, your total savings would be $2,366,220 and your heirs would receive $7,680,478.

Caution

Protect Your Assets

Making money is important, but keeping it is just as important. You need to properly protect your assets including your trading account. I have added *Appendix B* for this very reason. I learned the hard way; I did not know how to protect what I worked so hard for and that one mistake cost me a lot. Please read this brief section carefully and educate yourself on this very important aspect of investing. To read more, visit www.traderslibrary.com/TLEcorner.

You should now have a much better idea of the importance of a financial blue print. As a final lesson, I want you to notice that the interest rate in retirement examples five and six was an average of 15% during the 20-year time frame from the age 40 to the age 60 while the average rate of return was 10% during your 18-year retirement, ages 60 to 78. The point I want to express to you is two-fold: first, if you don't have a plan, you'll financially be in trouble later on in life; and second, if you don't achieve the right rate of return and get started at an early age, you may never reach your financial goal. While this example is strictly for educational purposes only, I think you can see how important it is to increase your rate of return both pre-retirement and post-retirement. It's now time for you to begin increasing your rate of return with the use of options.

Big Money, Less Risk

Trade Options

One
Pointing the Way
with Technical Indicators

IN THIS CHAPTER

Examining support and resistance
The power of moving averages
Discovering Average True Range and Inertia
Combining indicators for effective trading

I'M A STRONG BELIEVER that your success with options is contingent on the use of technical indicators, which is why I chose to start the book here. This chapter will outline some of the many technical indicators that you can use within the market. We will go through the basics such as support and resistance levels, moving averages, Stochastics, and MACD. We will also head further into advanced technical indicators such as Bollinger Bands, Fibonacci retracements, Ease of Movement, Inertia, and Average True Range (ATR). The more indicators you have within your tool box, the better prepared you'll be for any market condition or type of trade. Mastering these technical skills will be necessary for you to become a successful options trader.

SUPPORT AND RESISTANCE LEVELS

There are price points when stocks will often make a change in direction and move from an upward direction (resistance) to a downward direction (support) and vice versa from support to resistance.

Keep in mind that an old resistance level will become the new support level when the movement is breaking upward and old support will become new resistance in a downward trend. Let's look at a few charts that highlight these levels of support and resistance.

Figure 1.1 shows both the support and resistance levels, beginning with resistance on the left side. Our chart shows that when the stock was moving higher, it reached a level of resistance, which you'll notice was established at the price of $100. Once the stock broke up through this resistance level of $100 (which is often on increased volume), the stock continued higher until reaching a high of $130, which again became resistance. After the stock reached $130, the price dropped back to the $100 level (old resistance now new support) where it finally on the third attempt failed to stay above $100 (support) and dropped to about $80 per share.

FIGURE 1.1 — — — | Support Level —

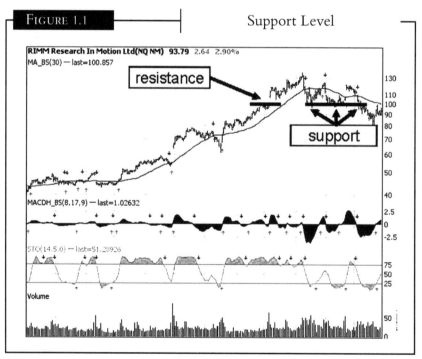

For color charts go to: www.traderslibrary.com/TLECorner • Chart by: thinkorswim.com

MOVING AVERAGES

Moving averages are price indications as to what the average price of the stock is over a certain given time frame. For example, let's begin with a 30-day simple moving average; it represents the average price of the stock for the last 30 days. As a trader, moving averages are helpful in many ways, but we use them primarily to determine our entry or exit points.

During an uptrend (Figure 1.2), the 30-day moving average acts as a support level and as long as the stock price remains above this level, the stock should continue back up. If you look at Figure 1.3, you'll notice that when stock price does not stay above the 30-day moving average, it drops further down and even faster than when it went up. When the stock does begin its next upward movement,

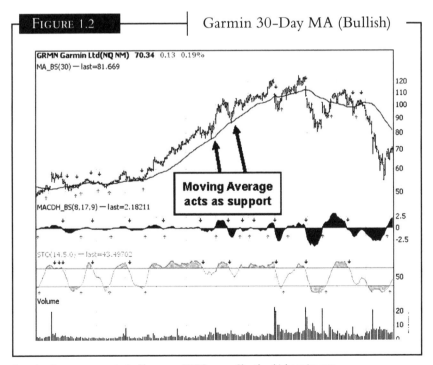

FIGURE 1.2 — Garmin 30-Day MA (Bullish)

For color charts go to: www.traderslibrary.com/TLECorner • Chart by: thinkorswim.com

it will more than likely have a tough time getting above the 30-day moving average because what was support will often become resistance. With this example we were using a 30-day moving average as short-term support and resistance levels. In the next example, you'll see how we can use multiple moving averages like the 30-, 50-, 100-, and 200-day moving averages.

MULTIPLE MOVING AVERAGES

Using several moving averages helps us determine what the next point of support or resistance will be. It's said that when a stock drops below its 30-day support level, it will move towards its 50-day moving average, which will be another level of support. When breaking that level, it will test its 100-day and then final-

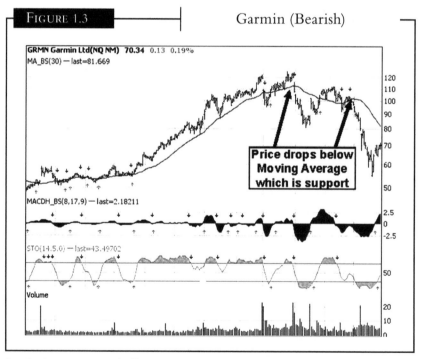

FIGURE 1.3 — Garmin (Bearish)

For color charts go to: www.traderslibrary.com/TLECorner • Chart by: thinkorswim.com

4

ly its 200-day moving average. When the stock drops below it's 200-day moving average, which is referred as the strongest point of support (on downward moving stocks), the stock has broken its long-term support and now its downward trend will increase even more. This 200-day moving average acts the opposite when stocks are moving off of their lows and heading up because the 200-day is now resistance. If the stock can increase above this level, it is considered a very bullish sign and the stock now has great upside potential. I'm going to begin showing you several different charts with four moving averages.

As you can see in Figure 1.4 for the S&P 500 we have four different settings, 30-, 50-, 100-, and the 200-day moving average. When I trade, I use various colors to set up my moving averages

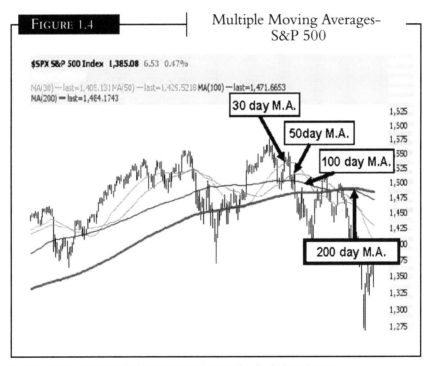

FIGURE 1.4 Multiple Moving Averages- S&P 500

For color charts go to: www.traderslibrary.com/TLECorner • Chart by: thinkorswim.com

5

so I know which ones are which (on this chart they are labeled for you). For example the 30-day moving average is the short-term support level if the stock is above it and is short-term resistance if the stock is below. The 50- and 100-day moving averages are the next points of support when trending down. The all-important 200-day moving average is the long-term support level for any stock or index. Keep in mind that these are levels of resistance as stocks or indexes move upwards.

If you take a quick snapshot of the S&P 500 chart (Figure 1.4), you'll see that when the price of the index is above all four moving averages, then the index has a tendency to be bullish and move upward; yet, when the price of the index begins dropping below the 30-day moving average, we see our first signs of weakness (you should begin to determine your exit or place stop losses now). At this point, the index will tend to move to the next level of support, which will be the 50-day. If it can stop at that level, it will move higher, making the 30-day the resistance level; however, when it drops below the 50-day, it's going to move towards the 100-day and look for support. If it cannot stop (which it did not in this example), the index will drop towards the 200-day and if this fails,

> **INSIDER SECRET**
>
> Think of each moving average as a different testing level of support (on downward moving stocks) or resistance (on upward moving stocks). The stock or index will keep pushing in its given direction until one of these levels of moving averages stops it. If none of them hold, then you can be sure that the movement of the stock will be strong in its original direction.
>
> As a general rule, when long the market, you want prices to stay above these moving averages and when short, you want prices to stay below them.

then you know you'll have the greatest odds of a bearish downward move.

I know it sounds confusing, so let's look at a second and third example. We'll review the Russell 2000 index (Figure 1.5) and GRMN (Figure 1.6) to simplify the importance of the multiple moving averages.

Looking at the example of the Russell 2000 index (Figure 1.5), you'll notice several points of interest. First, I always like to determine the long-term one year support and resistance levels, which are not just based on the use of moving averages but also on the highs and lows of the 12-month chart (as we talked about earlier).

We determined the resistance (ceiling) was the 850 point because the index could not move above this area after making several at-

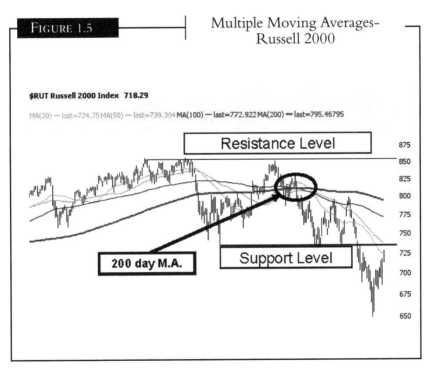

FIGURE 1.5   Multiple Moving Averages– Russell 2000

$RUT Russell 2000 Index 718.29

MA(30) — last=724.75 MA(50) — last=739.304 MA(100) — last=772.922 MA(200) — last=795.46795

Resistance Level

200 day M.A.   Support Level

For color charts go to: www.traderslibrary.com/TLECorner • Chart by: thinkorswim.com

tempts to do so. The support level (floor) was between 725 and 750, so we'll call it 735. Now that we know what to expect during a bullish and bearish move, let's look at the location of the index price in relationship to the four different moving averages.

The last time the index attempted to move through its resistance of 850, it failed and began a bearish downward movement. It attempted to move higher afterwards; but, if you'll look at the chart, you'll notice I circled the four moving averages showing the price of the index (800) was below these moving averages. It was also below the 200-day moving average, which is a very bearish sign. The index then dropped 150 points to about 650 before finding new support.

WATCH BREAKS OF THE 200-DAY MOVING AVERAGE

To give you an idea of how far this drop was, the Dow Jones would need to drop about 100 points for the Russell 2000 to drop 15 points; so, the 150 point drop in the Russell 2000 amounted to 1500 points within the Dow Jones. By the way, this also occurred within 15 days. So before I move on to an example of multiple moving averages on the stock Garmin, let me give you a final thought about the importance of using four moving averages. If stocks or indexes are moving up, you want the prices to be above these moving averages; however, when the price drops below the 30-day, you'd better know your exit because if the price drops below the 50, then it's going to the 100-day. If it drops below the 200-day, it's "good night Irene" (a saying from a favorite movie of mine *The Perfect Storm*). You'll see not only the largest but often the fastest drop beginning the day that happens, and if you don't know how to weather this type of storm, you'll be seeing a huge drop within your portfolio. Also, if you're seeing the prices of the major index such as the QQQQ (Powershares), $RUT (Russell 2000), $INDU (Dow Jones), or $SPX (Standard and Poors 500) drop below their 200-day moving averages, it may be a good time to close out your mutual funds, go to a cash fund, and weather out the storm until you have bullish buy signals within these major indexes.

SUMMARIZING THE USES OF MOVING AVERAGES

Looking at the GRMN chart (Figure 1.6) you'll notice I have placed four numbers within the chart. Let's review these four numbers in detail so you'll have a greater understanding of how important the use of various moving averages can be.

Beginning with number 1, you'll see that the price of the stock was above the moving averages at about $55 per share and continued

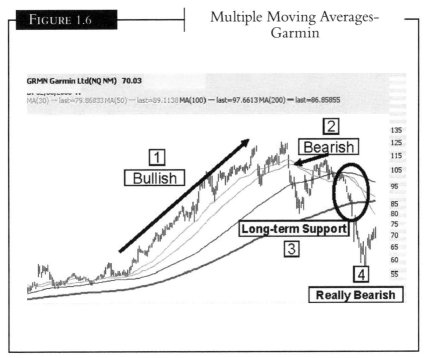

| FIGURE 1.6 | Multiple Moving Averages-Garmin |

For color charts go to: www.traderslibrary.com/TLECorner • Chart by: thinkorswim.com

above them until reaching a price of $125. At this time the price dropped below the top moving average (30-day) and then the second moving average (50-day) and stopped at $95 per share before moving back up to $125 per share. So what just happened?

The stock reached a price resistance level of $125, failed to break up through that price, and pulled back down to $95, stopping at that level and not moving towards the next lowest moving average of 100 or even worse, the 200. If the price dropped below the 100-day moving average, its natural reaction is to go to the long-term support level of 200 and, if failing that, (go ahead and say it) "good night Irene."

Before you read on, let's add more value by asking one simple question: if you were to buy the stock (or call option) when the stock was trading at about $55 per share, when would you have exited the trade and taken your profit? Would you have sold when the stock was at $65, $75, $85, $100, $110, $125, or would you still be in the trade when it's at $70? Any answer would be correct because you would have made a profit and as the saying goes, "you can't go broke taking a profit."

How about exiting the trade when the stock reached $105 per share? Why that price instead of some other price? In my mind, it was just time to "do it"! Look at Figure 1.7 and notice that this is when the 10-day moving average dropped below the 20-day, which is a sign of weakness and possibly a bearish downward move. If that wasn't an exit opportunity for you, then you would have been praying you had a stop loss in place because while the stock did move back up to the $125 resistance level, it failed to go higher and dropped to $75 per share.

If you were using the Average True Range indicator (which we will discuss later in this chapter) as a tool for placing stop loss orders, your exit price would have been $115 per share, which is still

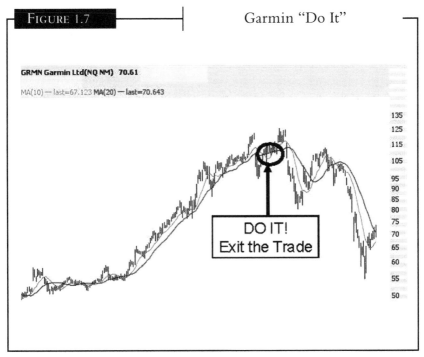

FIGURE 1.7 — Garmin "Do It"

For color charts go to: www.traderslibrary.com/TLECorner • Chart by: thinkorswim.com

better than watching the stock drop to $75 or owning the stock at $70 per share. I'm excited to share my knowledge of the Average True Range indicator (ATR). If you're new to the market, you probably don't know much about stop loss orders; and if you're an experienced trader, you may not be using stop loss orders because you've been burned in the past. Get over it, because it will happen again; however, with the use of the ATR, your odds of it happening as often will dramatically decrease.

THE "DO IT" INDICATOR

As more of a short-term trader I use a combination of a 10- and a 20-day simple moving average to help determine the stock's current momentum (bullish or bearish). I actually refer to these set-

Simple versus Exponential

The difference between a simple and an exponential moving average is in how each stock price is weighted. In a simple moving average, the stock prices used in the specific time period are all given the same weight. With an exponentially weighted moving average, the latest data is given more weight. For this reason, an exponential moving average tends to react quicker; however, when you hear the term "moving average" it is most likely referring to the simple calculation. (Source: Investopedia.com)

tings as my "Do It" indicators because if I have not made my decision after reviewing various other technical indicators and price patterns, this gives me the confidence to pull the trigger (Do It) and place the trade.

I wish I could say that I thought of the name but it actually came from Carol and Osvaldo, who were great students and are now good friends. Carol once said, "if I wasn't sure what to do after looking at other technical indicators, I would look at the crossing of the two moving averages (10 and 20) and feel better about what direction the stock was moving," then place the trade accordingly (Do It).

By watching the crossing of the 10 and 20, we're able to determine a better entry and exit point for the trade as well as determine if the stock or overall market has current bullish or bearish momentum. Next, we're going to examine the details of buy and sell signals. First, I will cover the bullish entry showing the 10- and 20-day simple moving averages as they head higher. Then, we'll cover the bearish exit showing the 10- and 20-day moving lower. Again, these are indicators that help a trader better determine the short-term visual of the investment; it's up to you to determine what investment strategy to utilize—and that's where the rest of this book will come into play. Later on, I will teach you the particular option strategies that will work best under different market conditions.

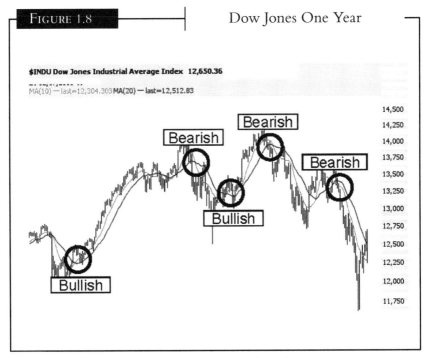

FIGURE 1.8 ——————|————— Dow Jones One Year ——

$INDU Dow Jones Industrial Average Index 12,650.36

MA(10) — last=12,304.303 MA(20) — last=12,512.83

For color charts go to: www.traderslibrary.com/TLECorner • Chart by: thinkorswim.com

On this one year Dow Jones chart (Figure 1.8), you can see the bullish and bearish markings I've added. More important, you can see that every time the Dow Jones showed great upside potential, the faster 10-day moving average moved up through the slower 20-day moving average and resulted in a bullish entry point.

Let's put some numbers to the chart and say that the Dow Jones was trading between 12,000 and 12,250 at the time of the upward crossing, because at that bullish signal the Dow Jones moved up to a price of about 13,500. Knowing this increase of at least 1,250 points for the Dow Jones before the crossing meant that you could have profited on bullish investments on stocks that trade within the Dow Jones. Or, as an option trader, you could have purchased call options on the DIA (diamonds), which is an Exchange Traded Fund (ETF).

Of course, what goes up must come down. Let's look at the far right side of the same chart. You'll see that later that year, the 10-day crossed below the 20-day moving average as the Dow Jones dropped from a price of 13,250 to 11,750, for a drop of 1,500 points in 1 month. This was the time I began writing this book, and it indicated that this may be another really bearish market. Whether I'm right or wrong about the future direction of the market, I can say this right now, "I would not want to own stocks within the Dow Jones after the crossing of the 10-day moving average began at 13,250."

Also you'll notice several other times when the index was bullish and bearish throughout the year. If you're a buy and hold long-term investor, then you may not use these type of technical settings; but, if you're a shorter-term trader using your "get rich" bag of money, then these indicators will help you select the best timing opportunity based on the odds of the market going higher or lower.

These indicators will help you select the best timing opportunity based on the odds of the market going higher or lower.

MULTIPLE USES FOR THE "DO IT" INDICATOR

I'm now going to show you how the "DO IT" indicator could benefit you in determining when to enter and exit single stocks and in understanding how the signals will give you a better feeling about a company's earnings before their release. That's correct; you may use the same process to evaluate a stock to determine if they will have good or bad earnings and be able to exit the trade to avoid larger drops if the company's earnings are disappointing. Take a look at the chart for Apple Computers (Figure 1.9) and you'll be amazed at how powerful the use of technical indicators can be.

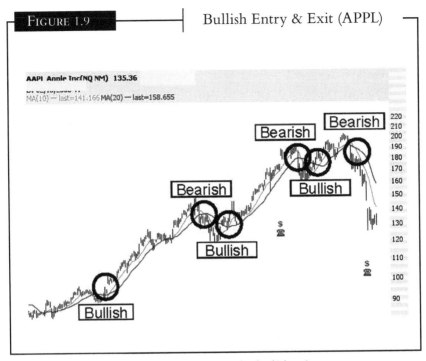

| FIGURE 1.9 | Bullish Entry & Exit (APPL) |

For color charts go to: www.traderslibrary.com/TLECorner • Chart by: thinkorswim.com

Using shorter-term moving averages and their crossings, let's compare the three different buy and sell opportunities versus the buy and hold opportunities. As you'll see, each time the 10-day moving average crossed through the 20-day moving average, the stock showed greater signs of bullishness. Each time the 10-day moving average crossed below the 20-day moving average, the stock showed signs of being bearish (Figure 1.9). Taking this information and using it to our advantage, look at our buy and sell opportunities:

1. Buy @ $95 – Sell @ $135 = 40 points
2. Buy @ $135 – Sell @ $170 = 35 points
3. Buy @ $180 – Sell @ $185 = 5 points

With the use of these two moving averages, you were able to identify better buy and sell opportunities, which totaled 3 trades for a profit of 80 points during the 12-month time frame. If you bought Apple at $95 and still owned it 12 months later, your profit would be 40 points ($135 - $95 = 40 points). By using the "Do It" indicator instead of buy and hold, you earned double the return with less risk.

Look at Figure 1.10. There are dollar sign symbols that represent the release of the company's earnings. I'd ask myself, "is the 10-day moving average above the 20-day before the company releases its earnings?" Looking at the two different earnings release icons ($) for Apple, you'll notice that Apple did move higher in the first example (number one) but dropped over 60 points prior to its next earnings release (example two).

Let's take a closer look. Number 1: The 10-day was above the 20-day moving average, which occurred at the $130 price. This is a bullish upward signal. If I were long the market during the release of the company's earnings, this would help me feel much more comfortable about doing so because the 10 stayed above the 20 going into the release of earnings. Number 2: The 10-day was below the 20-day at the price of $190, which is a bearish downward signal. This is a good sign that once the company releases its earnings, it may go much further down, which was indeed the case with Apple. This stock dropped $30 when earnings were released and continued down to the $120 price before finding its level of support and moving higher.

Will these two moving averages always tell us if the company's earnings will be good or bad? No, but again I use these indicators to show the current momentum of the stock: 10 above 20 is bullish momentum; 10 below 20 is bearish momentum.

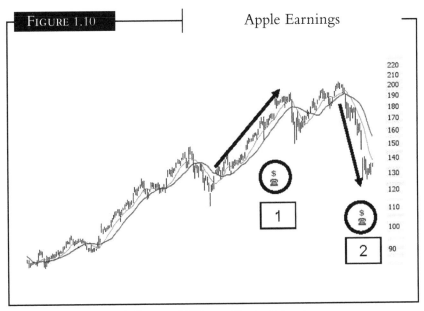

For color charts go to: www.traderslibrary.com/TLECorner • Chart by: thinkorswim.com

With the use of these two moving averages, you should always be prepared to make some type of a decision. If you're not going to sell when the 10 crosses below the 20, then you should at least place a stop loss to avoid bigger losses. I'll cover a great technical indicator known as ATR (Average Trading Range) later in this chapter so you'll be able to really fine tune your stop loss orders.

Just for the sake of you Google lovers, let's see how beneficial the same indicator settings would have worked during Google's earnings (Figure 1.11). Number 1: The 10-day was above the 20-day, which began at the $525 price and continued up to about $750 before the 10-day crossed down.

INSIDER SECRET

The crossing of the 10- and 20-day moving averages is an extremely useful indicator. Remember, the 10 above the 20 means bullish momentum; and the 10 below the 20 is bearish momentum.

17

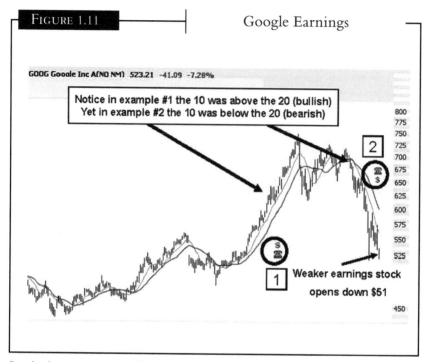

FIGURE 1.11 — Google Earnings

GOOG Gooale Inc A(NO NM) 523.21 -41.09 -7.28%

Notice in example #1 the 10 was above the 20 (bullish)
Yet in example #2 the 10 was below the 20 (bearish)

2

1

Weaker earnings stock
opens down $51

For color charts go to: www.traderslibrary.com/TLECorner • Chart by: thinkorswim.com

More important, prior to the company's next earnings release (represented by Number 2), the stock began a downward movement as the 10-day crossed below the 20-day at the $675 price. The day after earnings were released, the stock traded down another $51 to a price of $512.

Using these indicators, you would have done one of three things at the $675 price; you could have 1) exited the bullish trades, 2) placed a stop loss, or 3) even better yet, took on a bearish trade with the purchase of a put option.

FIBONACCI RETRACEMENTS

Fibonacci retracements are technical analysis tools that show the likelihood of an investment price retracing a large portion of an original move to find support or resistance at key Fibonacci levels before continuing in the original direction. These levels are created by drawing a trend line between two extreme points and then dividing the vertical distance by the key Fibonacci ratios of 23.6%, 38.2%, 50%, 61.8% and 100%.

LINGO

Fibonacci Numbers and Ratios

The Fibonacci number sequence was discovered by Leonardo de Pisa. The first number is a 0, the second a 1, and each subsequent number is generated by taking the sum of the two preceding it. Here's how the first part of the Fibonacci sequence looks: 0,1,1,2,3,5,8,13,21, 34, 55, 89, 144, 233, 377, 610, 987, and so forth to infinity.

Traders use the mathematical relationships between the numbers to help determine retracements and support and resistance. Some of the key numbers for retracement studies are:

- **1.618:** approximately how many times greater each number is from the one before it.
- **61.8%:** found by dividing one number by the one that follows it. This is the "Golden Ratio," which has many occurrences in nature.
- **38.2%:** found by dividing one number by the number two places to the right of it.
- **23.6%:** found by dividing one number by the one that is three places to the right of it.

(For more information, please visit www.investopedia.com)

Fibonacci retracements are popular tools used by many technical traders to help identify strategic places for transactions, target prices, or stop losses. As you'll see in Figure 1.12, we have drawn a Fibonacci retracement using a one-year chart beginning at the extreme low of about 12,000 and drawing upwards to the extreme high of about 14,200. Using this example, you'll notice that after the Dow Jones reached its high, it began a downward move. During this time, an investor educated in Fibonacci would anticipate the Dow Jones stopping at the 23.6%, 38.2%, 50%, 61.8% or 100% retracement levels before beginning an upward move again.

This was not the case with the Dow Jones because as the price reached each of these levels, it only continued down showing greater signs of bearish momentum. Now that you can identify the weakness as the Dow Jones moves below these retracement levels, you can determine your exit point just below any of the five retracement levels, which is often once the investment breaks down through the 23.6% level. It is said that if the investment, in this case the Dow Jones, drops down through the 50% retracement, then the drop will only be intensified with a faster downward drop. The

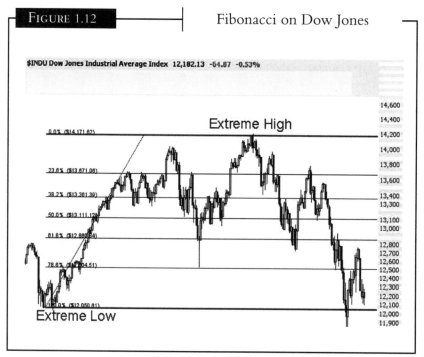

FIGURE 1.12   Fibonacci on Dow Jones

$INDU Dow Jones Industrial Average Index 12,182.13 -64.87 -0.53%

For color charts go to: www.traderslibrary.com/TLECorner • Chart by: thinkorswim.com

Fibonacci retracements can also be used to help determine resistance on an upward level after testing the lower retracement.

Figure 1.13 shows a Fibonacci retracement on a stock, and as with the previous example, we've drawn the retracement line from the extreme low to the extreme high using a one-year chart. The important lesson to learn here is that the price of $100 became an area of resistance on the way up and, after reaching higher highs and drawing the retracement, this area was the 38.2% retracement on the way down (support). Once failing this level and dropping to a lower retracement level, this 38.2% retracement becomes resistance on the way up (this can be seen within the boxed section A).

It is extremely common for prices to react this way at certain retracement levels especially if the retracement level is formed at

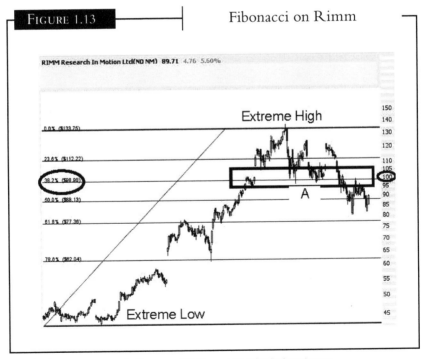

FIGURE 1.13 — Fibonacci on Rimm

For color charts go to: www.traderslibrary.com/TLECorner • Chart by: thinkorswim.com

price points such as $100. These price points and retracement levels often become major areas of support on downward trends and major areas of resistance on upward trends. This is similar to how we use multiple moving averages. If you like Fibonacci Retracements, then you need to pick up the book *Chart Your Way to Profits* by Tim Knight (founder of Prophet.net) and read about the powerful Fibonacci Fans.

AVERAGE TRUE RANGE INDICATOR (ATR)

If you have ever placed a stop loss on an investment, you'll know how important it is to determine an appropriate price to help avoid selling too soon or too late. This by far has to be one of my favorite tools for helping determine a stop loss price for either the stock or option. Let's begin with a simple explanation of the Average True Range (ATR), which settings work best, and why various investments will require different settings.

The true range indicator is the greatest of the following: the absolute value of the current high less the previous close or the absolute value of the current low less the previous close.

If you understand that equation, then good for you! In my opinion, I don't need to know the math, I just need to know how to use it and more important, how it can benefit my trades. I will start with an example of a very expensive stock (Google), then go to a much cheaper stock (Boeing). Finally, I'll share with you my personal secret on how to use the ATR as a stop loss for my directional (calls and puts) option trades.

EXAMPLE 1 – GOOGLE

Figure 1.14 of Google shows a current ATR setting of (14) and a last price of 24.51 (bottom left side of chart), which really means

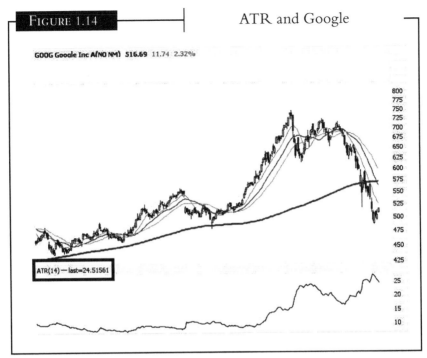

that for the past 14 trading days Google's average daily trading range has been about $24.51 per day. That's correct; its recent average daily movement up or down is about $24.51. You may be wondering how this will benefit you as a trader. Well, whether you're a stock investor or option investor, you know now that you should be willing to give up $24.51.

For example, say the stock closed today at $525 per share and you wanted to place a stop loss because it's been moving down a lot recently (seen in the right side of the chart). You would need to place your stop loss at a price greater than $24.51. To calculate—subtract $24.51 from the stock price of $525 so your stop loss would be set at the price of $500.49. Be careful though—$500 can be a huge level of support. You might want to place the stop loss a few dollars below $500 to allow your stop loss to be just below support and not above it.

A $24.51 stop loss is large; however, if you look at this next example (Figure 1.15) of Google, you'll see that during the bullish upward trend the ATR had a daily average of $13.98. The ATR number tells us that during this upward bullish trend, the stock moves less on average. Your stop loss will be lower to allow for less of a loss during the upward trend. Note that the ATR increased to a daily average of $24.51 during the downward trend; again confirming that stock prices drop faster when going down and move up slower when bullish.

You may want to also make note that the ATR chart (across the bottom) shows the average price throughout the chart along with various numbers on the right side (10,15,20,25), which you can use to see the average ATR price during the chart's time frame. Looking at the ATR line and referencing the various numbers on the

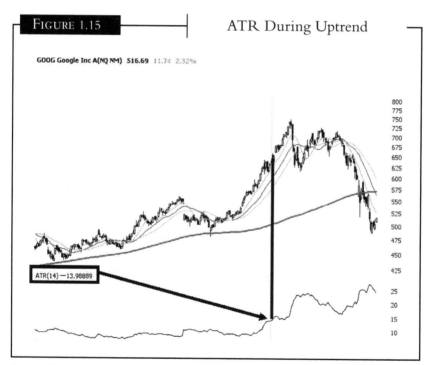

FIGURE 1.15   ATR During Uptrend

For color charts go to: www.traderslibrary.com/TLECorner • Chart by: thinkorswim.com

right side of the ATR chart, you can see the average ATR range during the entire 12 months. At certain times throughout the year the stock has a higher ATR while other times throughout the year it shows the ATR as being lower.

This could be that the stock itself or the stock market as a whole reacts differently during certain months of the year, which creates more volatility (movement) than average and, therefore, the ATR number fluctuates. The same applies to an individual stock during earnings; stocks tend to be more volatile going into earnings, which will increase the ATR. This is good because we'll be able to set proper stop loss expectations and hopefully avoid getting stopped out too early or at the wrong price.

EXAMPLE 2– BOEING

Looking at the ATR (14-day range) for Boeing, which is highlighted on the left side of the chart (Figure 1.16), we see a current price of $2.47. This number represents the average daily price movement for the past 14 trading days. Now it's up to you to decide if you're going to use a stop loss of $2.47 or double the ATR number and place a stop loss at $4.94.

In our previous example with Google, the stock recently had an ATR of $24.51, so doubling that number to about $49 is too large a number for a stop loss; but, with a less expensive stock such as Boeing, doubling the ATR would be a good idea. With the Boeing stock trad-

> **INSIDER SECRET**
>
> When using ATR to determine your stop loss, use the price of the stock to help determine if you should use the base number or if you should double it. With expensive stocks, the current ATR should be adequate, whereas with lower priced stocks (like Boeing), you may find that doubling it provides a better stop loss point.

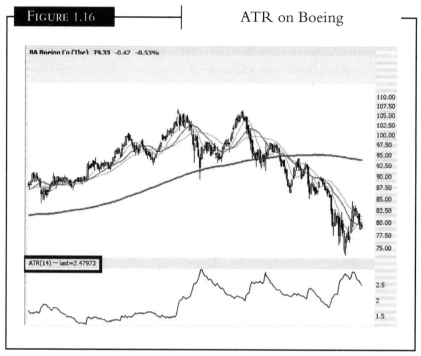

ing at $79, we would be setting a stop loss at about $74 per share, which is the current ATR of $2.47 doubled to about $5.

Now that we have discussed the use of ATR for both high and low priced stocks, let's give you a short example of using ATR with options. Taking the example of Boeing, let's say that you have established a price for the stop loss, which in this example we decided that $5 (or two times the current ATR of $2.47) below the current stock price was sufficient. We will place a contingent order to sell our option when the price of the stock reaches $74, which is $5 below the current price of the stock. Not all of your brokerage firms allow this type of execution order. If this is the case, you can also place the contingent order to sell your (call) option when the stock trades at the price of $74 per share. In short, we're agree-

Want More?

I hope that you'll take advantage of what you've learned here because the cost of this book has more than paid for itself with just this explanation of ATR. If you're really interested in seeing this in detail, invest in *The Complete Guide to Technical Indicators*, which is a complete 6 hour 4-DVD set of my favorite indicators such as Average True Range. The investment will be well worth it as I show you when to buy and when to sell, as well as which indicators work best and with which settings.

ing to sell our option at the bid price if the stock trades at a price of $74. As you'll learn later, if you're not willing to own the stock then don't bother owning a call option.

This type of decision making will help you become non-emotional about your investments and allow for a more consistent plan of action. If you were trading put options to invest in a stock dropping in value, then you would reverse your thought process and set a stop loss on your option when the stock moved up a certain amount. If your ATR was $3, you want to double that to $6 and place an order to sell the put option if the stock moves up $6 per share.

INERTIA INDICATOR

If I haven't used the word favorite, then allow me to do so here. Out of over 200 different type of technical indicators, I give the Inertia indicator the most credit for helping me determine when the markets or individual stocks are bullish or bearish. Developed in 1995, the Inertia indicator is relatively simple to interpret. If the Inertia indicator is above 50, it is known as positive inertia and it defines the long-term trend as up while the indicator remains above 50. If the Inertia indicator is below 50, it is known as negative inertia and it defines the long-term trend as down while the indicator remains below 50.

I think this indicator works similar to an American football game. If you were to place the football in the center of the field, the game's objective is to control the ball and move it into the end zone by keeping the momentum moving until you score (exit the trade). If at any time during possession of the ball you lose it, then the opposing team takes control and will attempt to move the ball to the opposite end zone. In trading, the two different teams are known as the bulls and the bears.

You want to move with the trend and as the Inertia moves up through 50, the odds of bullish momentum are great. Once the

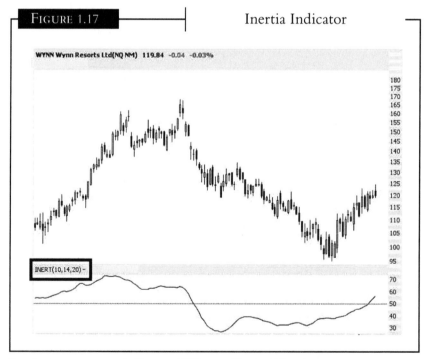

FIGURE 1.17   Inertia Indicator

For color charts go to: www.traderslibrary.com/TLECorner • Chart by: thinkorswim.com

momentum drops down through the 50, the momentum is now bearish with great odds of the market or stocks dropping.

Looking at Figure 1.17, you'll notice we are using the Inertia indicator with a setting of 10-14-20, which seems to work well for the indexes such as the Dow Jones, S&P 500, and Russell 2000. You'll also find that these settings actually work really well for stocks too. Now keep in mind that what works today doesn't mean it will work years from now; but, because this indicator is used as a long-term momentum indicator, you shouldn't need to change the settings that often. It is a good idea, however, to check that what worked today is still working months or even years from now.

Using the Inertia indicator with this stock, you'll see that there were two really nice moves up and down. With the use of the

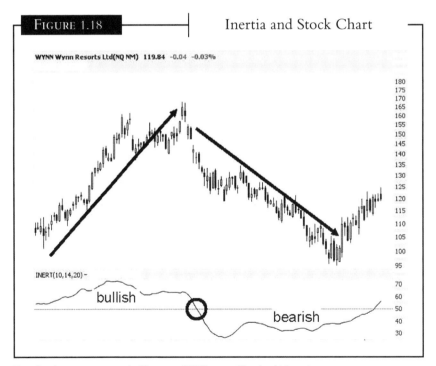

FIGURE 1.18 — Inertia and Stock Chart

For color charts go to: www.traderslibrary.com/TLECorner • Chart by: thinkorswim.com

indicator, you would have been able to benefit by using a bullish investment strategy when the stock moved up from $105 to $165 and by using a bearish strategy when it dropped from $150 to $95 (Figure 1.18).

Wouldn't it have been nice to know it was time to exit the trade at about $150 when the Inertia indicator crossed from positive to negative (seen within the circled area) instead of holding on to the stock and watching it drop back to $95 per share? This is a perfect example of why you need to trade both directions of the market and not just the up side. As I've said earlier, there isn't a stock from 1998 that I'd still be holding today because I would have lost a lot of money holding those stocks expecting that someday their value would be much greater.

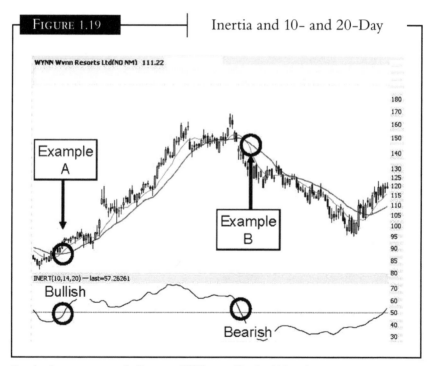

FIGURE 1.19 — Inertia and 10- and 20-Day

WYNN Wvnn Resorts Ltd(NO NM) 111.22

Example A

Example B

INERT(10,14,20) — last=57.26261

Bullish

Bearish

For color charts go to: www.traderslibrary.com/TLECorner • Chart by: thinkorswim.com

Now if you'll take this same example and add the 10- and 20-day simple moving average (the "Do It") settings to the chart, you would be able to better determine your buy and sell opportunities (Figure 1.19). Entering a bullish trade when the Do It crossed upward (example A), you would have seen an increase in the stock price from $90 to $170. When the Do It and Inertia gave you bearish signals (example B), you would have been stopped out of the trade at about $163 because the ATR showed a 14-day average price movement of $7 during the bullish move up. It was also possible to have placed a bearish trade as the stock dropped from the $140 range to $95 when both the Inertia crossed the center line and the 10- and 20-day simple moving average crossed downwards.

ADDING IT ALL UP

Now that you've had a chance to review the power of not just the Inertia indicator but also the support of the Do It settings, you should have less fear and more confidence about placing a trade. In this case, would have profited $73 per share during a 5-month time frame. You could have made even more if you traded the stock downwards (put option) from the $140 price to $95 price range before the Inertia moved back above the center (50) and the 10- and 20-day also crossed up.

You can't rely on just one or two indicators if you want to be really successful in the markets. You need to be able to understand and examine how they work together in order to find the highest probability trades.

Looking at the far right side of the Wynn chart, you may be thinking it is time to be bullish on the stock and that may be true; however, you have to beware of the 200-day moving average and how powerful it is because it can act as a stock's major support level (floor) or major resistance level (ceiling).

Looking at Figure 1.20, it should validate that you can't rely on just a few technical indicators if you're going to be really good at

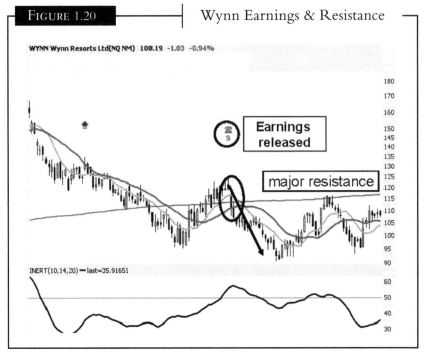

FIGURE 1.20 — Wynn Earnings & Resistance

For color charts go to: www.traderslibrary.com/TLECorner • Chart by: thinkorswim.com

trading the market up and down. You can see how the 200-day moving average affects the stock and why trading into an earnings release could increase your risk.

If you look carefully, you'll notice that the stock dropped on the release of its earnings, putting the price below the 200-day moving average, which now becomes a major level of resistance for the price as it moves upward. You can actually see that at the $115 price the stock failed to move higher through the resistance level (ceiling), dropped back down to the $95 price, and is currently trading at $108 per share.

I can't end this section without sharing why I said in the opening chapter that this would be the worst January in stock market history. If you'll look at Figure 1.21 you'll see the same two indica-

FIGURE 1.21 ──────────── Dow Jones Sell Off

For color charts go to: www.traderslibrary.com/TLECorner • Chart by: thinkorswim.com

(Bearish signals as the Dow Jones dropped from 13,250 to 11,600 at which time the 10 & 20 day Moving Average crossed down and the Inertia Indicator crossed down also)

tors we just referenced, Inertia and Do It, being used on the Dow Jones. This three-month chart shows bearish signals the first week of January. The information from these indicators gives you, the investor, the confidence to place stop losses on your stocks, exit your bullish option trades, and maybe even move your mutual funds into a cash type position as the Dow Jones quickly dropped 1,650 points from 13,250 to 11,600 in 20 days.

You should have no question that the Dow Jones is not ready to move much higher. One major sign is that the Inertia indicator is below the center line giving us a bearish signal.

Of the various chapters within this book, this section will by far give you the greatest opportunity to beat the market, and the rea-

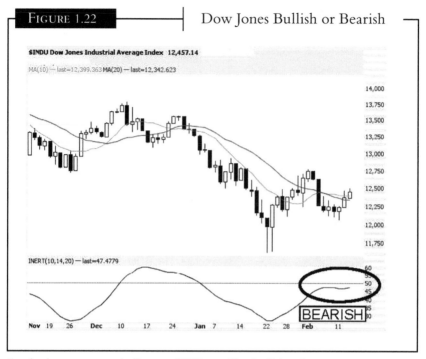

FIGURE 1.22 — Dow Jones Bullish or Bearish

For color charts go to: www.traderslibrary.com/TLECorner • Chart by: thinkorswim.com

Having patience is important as you'll see the Inertia Indicator is neither bullish nor bearish as it's trending sideways.

son I say that is because of timing. You can buy stock or trade options but your success will be dramatically increased by timing the investment opportunity and trading with the current market trends and not against them. Please keep in mind that life isn't perfect and nor will your trading decisions be, but the right tools and education will increase your odds of success and limit your losses.

There is no one strategy or indicator that I reference within my book that will give you the perfect buy or sell opportunity or the perfect buy or sell price, but do I think it will increase your odds of success? You better believe I do! It's why I've taken the time to write this book. It's about time you learn how to control your own financial future and join the 5% of people who will not rely on

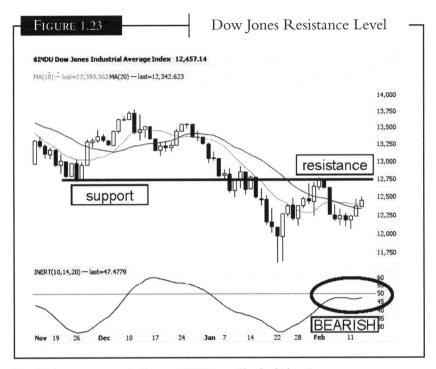

FIGURE 1.23 — Dow Jones Resistance Level

For color charts go to: www.traderslibrary.com/TLECorner • Chart by: thinkorswim.com

Dow Jones is showing strong Resistance at about 12,750 as the Inertia Indicator is still bearish as it remains below the center line.

Social Security or any other government subsidized income during retirement. Your money will be working for you instead of you working for your money.

Let's take one last look at the Inertia indicator (Figure 1.22). Is the Dow Jones bullish or bearish? If you're not sure, the answer is on the chart, and if you think it's moving much higher, look at one more chart (Figure 1.23). Studying technical indicators is extremely important to trading success—check out my DVD course *The Complete Guide to Technical Indicators* for more information. A review of the three different charts shows that you should have exited the market during the first few days of January. At this time, the Inertia indicator is below the "50 yard line" (center line) yet the 10- and 20-day moving averages are slightly bullish; however, if the Dow Jones does move higher, it will reach a level of resistance at 12,750 at which time, if it does not move higher, it will only move lower again until it finds another support level.

If it does break higher, its next level of resistance (ceiling) will be the 13,000 level, which is where the 200-day moving average is. Again, remember the 200-day moving average is a major level of support or resistance.

Whether you believe the chart is helping confirm that the market is neutral to bearish, we know one thing for sure: it's only bullish until it reaches 13,000, at which time we could see a change of direction. You'll want to focus on spread trades because your odds of success are much greater than if you were to purchase

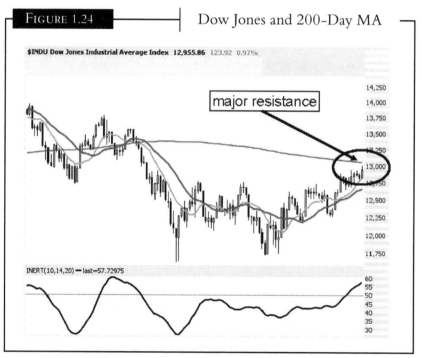

FIGURE 1.24 — Dow Jones and 200-Day MA

For color charts go to: www.traderslibrary.com/TLECorner • Chart by: thinkorswim.com

stocks or buy call options at this time. After looking at the Dow Jones and its 200-day moving average (Figure 1.24), I would choose to be in cash or willing to only hold conservative spread trades until the market makes its next decision to move higher and head back towards the all-time high of 14,200 or down to another level of support or new lows. The 13,000 level is a major level of resistance so unless it breaks up through this level, the markets will move sideways or down.

VOLATILITY INDEXES

If you're going to be an active trader, you'll need to have a better understanding of not just the various investment strategies or technical indicators but also the various volatility indexes such as the VIX, VXO, and VXN. We'll focus on the VIX indicator (the CBOE volatility index), which measures investor fear of a market decline. In general, volatility indexes are contrarian indicators (i.e. when the indexes are going down, the markets are rising. When the indexes are going up, the markets are falling).

When fear of a market decline is rising, traders generally begin selling positions and market prices tend to go down in response. When fear is subsiding or optimism is high, traders are buying and the market prices tend to rise

---

LINGO

VIX: The Chicago Board of Exchange (CBOE) volatility index based on the S&P 500.

VXO: The CBOE volatility index based on the S&P 100 (OEX).

VXN: The CBOE volatility index based on the NASDAQ.

(For more information see: The CBOE's website at http://www.cboe.com/micro/IndexSites.aspx)

---

in response. When the VIX is low and moving higher, investors tend to sell and when the VIX is high and moving lower, investors

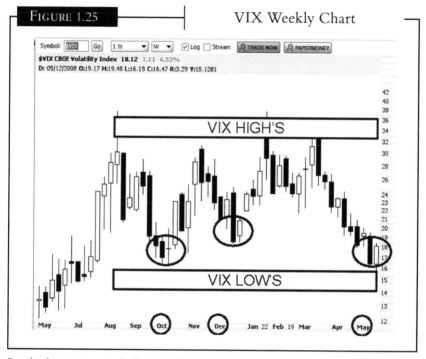

FIGURE 1.25 — VIX Weekly Chart

For color charts go to: www.traderslibrary.com/TLECorner • Chart by: thinkorswim.com

tend to buy. Hence the saying, "When the VIX is high, it is time to buy; and when the VIX is low, it is time to go."

The theory is that fear in the market should be at its highest when the stock prices are at their lowest (just prior to turning back up). Likewise, when the index is at its lowest point, market prices should be reaching a high (just before turning down). So theoretically, selling when the volatility index is low should result in selling at a market high. Buying when the volatility index is high should result in buying in at bottoming price levels.

Let's look at several charts to see how powerful the VIX indicator is when determining market highs and market lows. Keep in mind that when the VIX is high, the market tends to have less fear; and

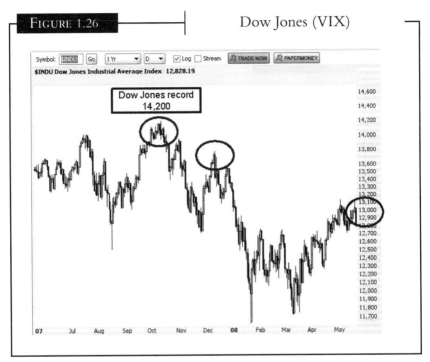

FIGURE 1.26 ——————| Dow Jones (VIX)

For color charts go to: www.traderslibrary.com/TLECorner • Chart by: thinkorswim.com

when the VIX is low, the market tends to have greater fear, which could be an early sign of market weakness.

Let's begin with Figure 1.25, which is a 12-month weekly chart of the VIX. As you'll notice within the circled areas, the VIX reached lows in October, December, and March, which again is a sign of weakness in the stock market. As the saying goes, "when it's low, look out below."

By looking at Figure 1.26, you'll see that during the three months of October, December, and January, the Dow Jones was higher before moving lower. As a perfect example you can see that the Dow Jones reached a record high of about 14,200 during October and at the same time the VIX was trading at its low of about 17.

39

Within the next 7 weeks, the Dow Jones dropped from its record high of about 14,200 to 12,700, resulting in a 1,500 point drop in that time frame.

I hope you'll never forget "when the VIX is high, it's time to buy; when the VIX is low, look out below." From this day forward, I encourage you to use the VIX indicator to plan your trades and more important, to plan the type of trades you should be placing based on the market's direction.

In our last example (Figure 1.27) we are comparing the VIX to the Dow Jones. Number one shows the Dow Jones at a high at the same time the VIX was at a low, which resulted in the Dow Jones making a large downward movement. Number two is the point where you can see the VIX at a high when the Dow Jones was at

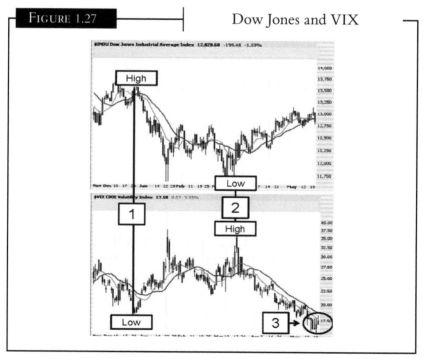

FIGURE 1.27 — Dow Jones and VIX

For color charts go to: www.traderslibrary.com/TLECorner • Chart by: thinkorswim.com

a low, which resulted in the Dow Jones rallying to the upside. At this point you shouldn't need to question how powerful the VIX is when it comes to timing the market. Be sure you're placing the correct trades based on the market's direction.

After clipping the charts above, the next day I decided to add a third example that shows the current VIX at about 17.50, which is below the previous VIX low of 18 back on December 24th. What happened today? Well, Figure 1.28 tells the story.

Looking back at Figure 1.27 and referring to number three, I had said that with the VIX being at a low, the Dow Jones could move even lower. And it did, moving down another 227 points and closing at the low of the day. This soon may mark the bottom of the market because the VIX moved up over one point on the day to

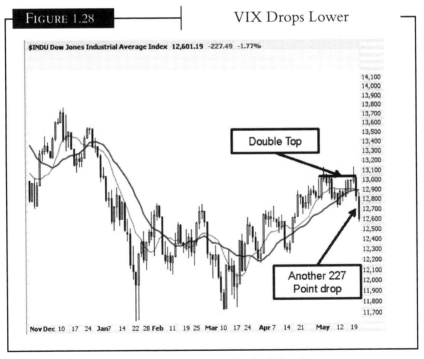

FIGURE 1.28 — VIX Drops Lower

For color charts go to: www.traderslibrary.com/TLECorner • Chart by: thinkorswim.com

41

18.59. It's now time to start selecting your investments and investment strategy based on the market's next move.

As I close out this section, I would like to encourage you to become more of a technical trader and not just a fundamental trader. Timing the market has to be by far the most important aspect of being successful. With the use of various technical indicators, you'll be able to reduce your fear and increase your confidence, which will create greater success. Keeping in mind that what goes up will go down, and the only way you'll know if your investments will drop is if you know how to use technical indicators to identify the changes. If you're looking to learn more about technical indicators, visit my website at www.whymoney.com and view the educational information I've made available.

I believe technical indicators are the key to perfecting your trading and building your confidence. Study chapter one thoroughly and you'll find that with the help of my favorite indicators, you'll be finding higher probability trades and winning more often.

Now that we have learned how to read the market, let's get started on our options education.

Self-test questions

1. Of the three different moving average settings, which one is referred to as the strongest point of support or resistance?

    A. 50-day moving average
    B. 100-day moving average
    C. 200-day moving average

2. The Average True Range Indicator works best to determine what?

    A. When to buy
    B. When to sell
    C. Where to place a stop loss

3. If a stock is about to reach a resistance level (ceiling), when would be the best time to buy?

    A. Before it breaks up through the resistance level
    B. After it breaks up through the resistance level with increased volume
    C. After it breaks up through the support level

4. Fibonacci Retracements are used to predict a stock's movement and during a downward movement, which of the three retracement levels is more important?

    A. 23% level
    B. 38% level
    C. 50% level

5. When using the Average True Range Indicator as a stop loss guide, it is best to double the 14-day average if the stock is very volatile and has a lot of movement.

  A. True
  B. False

6. With the use of a 10- and 20-day moving average, a stock tends to be more _____ when the 10-day crosses up through the 20-day.

  A. Bullish
  B. Bearish
  C. Neither

7. One of my favorite technical indicators is the Inertia Indicator, which works during what type of market?

  A. Upward Market
  B. Downward Market
  C. Both

8. My Inertia settings of choice are?

  A. 8, 14, 20
  B. 10, 14, 20
  C. 12, 14, 20

9. The Inertia Indicator works best to confirm which one of the three?

    A. Bullish upward movement

    B. Bearish downward movement

    C. A confirmation of a change from bullish to bearish or bearish to bullish.

10. When the VIX Indicator is low, it can be a sign that the market will move in which direction?

    A. Up

    B. Down

    C. Sideways

For answers, go to www.traderslibrary.com/TLEcorner.

Two

An Introduction to Options

IN THIS CHAPTER

Defining the parts of an option
Examining volume
Calculating implied volatility
Understanding at-, in-, and out-of-the-money options

OPTIONS ARE A FORM of leverage. If you ask any successful investor, whether it's in the stock market or real estate, it's best to use leverage as long as you know what you're doing and, worse case scenario, you know your maximum losses if your investment doesn't perform the way you expect it to. Options, if used properly, can help an investor in two main ways: 1) you can invest with less money than the cost of trading the stock, which creates less cash at risk and can generate larger rates of returns, and 2) you can even be wrong on the direction of the stock and still make money.

For example, during a bull market, an option investor will invest with the purchase of a call option, and as the underlying investment increases in value, so will the option value. We'll cover this in detail later.

On the other hand, bear markets, which many investors don't consider, can be the fastest way to make money. Historically, it takes the stock market longer to go up than it does down. When it drops, it does so four times as fast. Let's reference two past examples: first, the three-year bear market that began in April of 2000 and ended in April 2003 would have given you a great opportunity to use put options as a way to invest in a down market. Then, the market recovered starting in April 2003 to surpass the 1999 highs in mid-October 2007, which gave you a great opportunity to use call options as a bullish leverage investment.

LINGO

Option: An option is a contract giving the buyer the right, but not the obligation, to buy or sell an underlying asset at a specific price on or before a certain date. An option is a security, just like a stock or bond, and constitutes a binding contract with strictly defined terms and properties.

Call option: A call option gives its owner the right to buy the underlying security at a specific price for a limited period of time. As a rule, purchasers of call options are usually bullish while sellers are generally bearish.

Put option: A put option gives its owner the right to sell the underlying security at a specific price for a limited period of time. Buyers are generally bearish whereas sellers are expecting the market to turn bullish.

Options give you the ability to trade a bullish or bearish market with less out-of-pocket capital. We should begin this journey with the different parts of an option because if you make the wrong decision, then your option could end up worthless whether the market moved in your direction or not. When you purchase call or put options and the underlying stock moves in the direction you need it to, you still can lose money if it doesn't move far enough in the right direction. Now that doesn't apply to advanced options, which we'll cover in the later chapters. Advanced options involve putting two option trades together on the same stock to reduce the risk and to allow the underlying stock to go up, down, or sideways and still have a profitable trade.

Option Basics

As an options trader, you'll be trading stocks in groups of 100 shares, which is known as a contract. As the buyer of one call option contract, you have the right to purchase 100 shares of the underlying stock on or before your selected expiration date. Expiration day is when you must exercise your right to buy or sell the stock, which falls on the 3rd Friday of your chosen month. These expiration dates can be as recent as the current month or for many stock options expiration day can be as far out as two years from the current month (these are called LEAPS).

Before you can determine which option investment strategy will be best, you'll need to understand the basic terminology that makes up an option trade.

> **Caution**
>
> If you're new to options, you want to begin with single contracts of real money until you've perfected your technical analysis and timing, then increase the number of contracts. If you are going to begin with a small number of contracts, use a brokerage firm that will charge you for single contracts and not a single trade.

Strike Price

The term "strike price" is an exact chosen price at which you agree to buy or sell the underlying investment. Strike prices are determined by the actual current price of the underlying investment; stocks that trade within $5 to $25 have available strike prices in increments of $2.50.

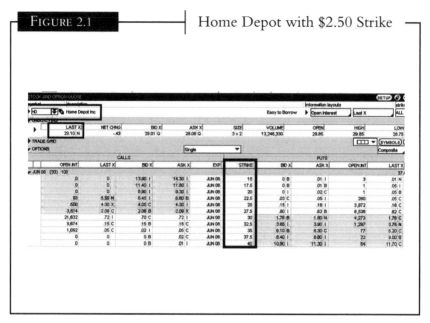

FIGURE 2.1 — Home Depot with $2.50 Strike

For color charts go to: www.traderslibrary.com/TLECorner • Chart by: thinkorswim.com

In Figure 2.1, the company Home Depot (ticker symbol HD) is trading at $29.10 per share; your choice for the July option strike prices would then range from $15 to $40 in increments of $2.50.

If you buy a call option at a strike price of $30, then you have the right to purchase the stock for $30 per share. If you write a covered call at the $40 strike price, you would be willing to sell your stock at the price of $40 per share. As another example, let's say you place a diagonal call spread of $50/$55, then you have the right to buy the underlying stock at $50 per share and to sell it for $55 per share, which would create a profit if the stock were to move above $55 per share. With many option strategies, we don't actually buy or sell the stock. We will close out our option trades prior to their expiration date for a profit or, in some cases, a loss. Either way, we still avoid having to tie up large amounts of money to trade the stock.

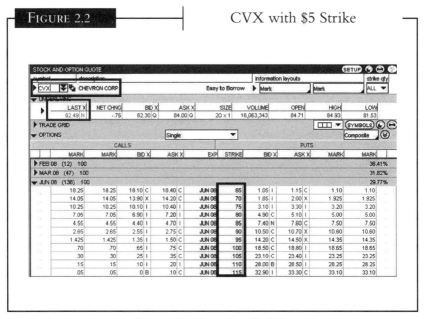

FIGURE 2.2 — CVX with $5 Strike

For color charts go to: www.traderslibrary.com/TLECorner • Chart by: thinkorswim.com

In the next strike price example we'll use the stock Chevron (CVX), which is trading at a price of $82.49. Looking at Figure 2.2, the strike prices for the month of May are in increments of $5, beginning with $65 and going to $115. As we said, stocks that trade within the $25 to $200 price range will have option strike prices in increments of $5.

In our last example (Figure 2.3) Google is trading at $515 per share, and the option strike prices are in increments of $10, beginning with $200 and going to a strike price of $580. Now, I've just shown you examples of three different stocks at three different prices with various strike prices. What you need to understand is that we can only choose from what is available and your strike price of choice will be based on your investment strategy.

Strike Price Changes

Beginning in the year 2008, the option markets began changing strike prices on certain stock; so, many stocks in the $5 to $25 range will have single dollar strikes, such as MSFT and many other stocks. This change is creating more opportunity for experienced option traders who know how to use these tighter strike prices to their advantage. You'll also see that certain stocks above $25 will have various strike prices that are not just in $5 increments; they too may offer single dollar strike prices. In the near future, we could even see tighter strike prices for the expensive stocks that are above $200.

Strike Prices (sample numbers)*
Underlying Investment under $25: Strike Price $2.50
Underlying Investment between $25-200: Strike Price $5
Underlying Investment over $200: Strike Price $10 or higher

*As the options markets change to meet the demands of current investors, you could see single dollar strike prices, even on expensive stocks. Also, when stocks split, you will see the strike price divide equally according to the amount of the split.

As you read on, keep in mind that a strike price is your chosen price at which you agree to trade an option whether it is a call or put option for a short-term current expiration or long-term, two-year expiration. Sometimes you'll see strike prices that are different than the examples here if the company has a recent stock split because option strike prices split according to a stock's split ratio. If your company was trading at $103 and split 3:1, your option would split equally. This means

We can only choose strike prices from what is available and your strike price of choice will be based on your investment strategy.

a $110 strike price will become a $36.67 strike price. If you're not sure of something, then my advice is to have a good coach to assist

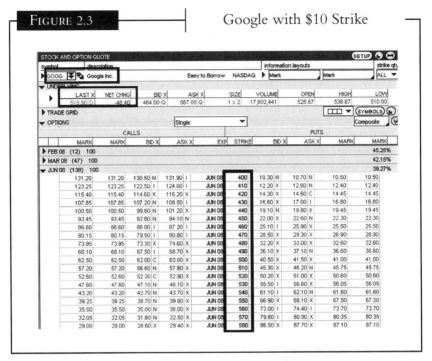

FIGURE 2.3 — Google with $10 Strike

For color charts go to: www.traderslibrary.com/TLECorner • Chart by: thinkorswim.com

you or to pick up the phone and call the trade desk at your broker-age firm.

EXPIRATION DATES

Options expire noon on the 3rd Saturday of any chosen month. Because you and I cannot trade after the market closes Friday 4 p.m. EST, we must exit our option trade by the close of the market on Friday. There are a few exceptions where expiration of options are the third Thursday of each month and even some that expire based on the opening of the price the morning of the third Friday of each month; however, that is only a few of the indexes such as the Russell 2000. Other than the small group of indexes, 99% of all options expire on the third Friday of your selected month, which even applies to an option on a stock that has an expiration of two years of more.

Let's say it's January 13th and the third Friday of January falls on January the 18th. This allows you only 5 days before the option expires. If that was the case and you were looking to purchase a call option to profit from an upward move or a put option to profit on a down move, then you wouldn't trade the current January option because there isn't enough time for the stock to move without risking the cost of the option.

As a guideline, when purchasing call or put options, I always consider purchasing an option that has three or more months of time before its expiration date. If I'm really positive the stock will move in my direction of choice on a longer time frame, then I would consider an option of six months to two years.

You'll also need to remember that not every stock offers an expiration date for every month for the next two years. For example, looking at Figure 2.4 you'll notice that the months of May and June, as well as several other months later in the year, are missing; yet, you'll find long-term options for January 2009 and January 2010, which are known as LEAPS.

Keep this simple: options roll out in a cycle. Do we care what the cycle is? No, just know you can only choose from what is available. It is important to know that there will always be options available for the current month; so, in Figure 2.4, we see February and March are available but no May or June yet. When we reach the month of April, the May options will be available. Remember, you will always be able to trade the cur-

> **INSIDER SECRET**
>
> As a guideline, when purchasing call or put options, I always consider purchasing an option that has three or more months of time before its expiration date.

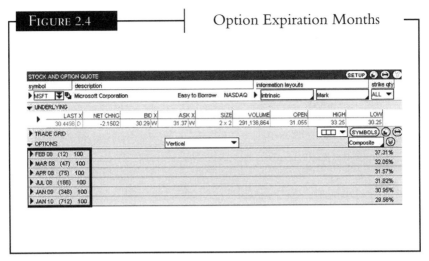

FIGURE 2.4 — Option Expiration Months

For color charts go to: www.traderslibrary.com/TLECorner • Chart by: thinkorswim.com

rent month; you just can't pick your own expiration month unless it's available.

INTRINSIC VALUE

We refer to intrinsic value as equity, which represents how much of your option cost is actually part of the option value. Using a real estate example may make more sense; think of intrinsic value as the equity portion of your lease option. Say you purchase a lease option on a home with a value of $250,000 and at the time of the lease option purchase, you pay $5,000 to have the right to purchase the home for $500,000 on or before a certain date. During the option period, the home value increased from $250,000 to a current value of $300,000. Your intrinsic value is now $50,000, which is determined by subtracting the current value of $300,000 from the option contract price of $250,000.

Let's now use an example of a stock to determine how much the option's intrinsic value would be. If you refer to Figure 2.5, you'll see that we have selected a call option strike price of $100, which

FIGURE 2.5   Intrinsic Value Call Option

		Calls								Puts				
Symbol	Last	Intrinsic Value	Bid	Ask	Vol	Open Interest	Strike	Symbol	Last	Intrinsic Value	Bid	Ask	Vol	Open Interest
IBM-CL	49.00	49.08	48.80	49.20	0	0	60.00	IBM-OL	0.05	0.00	N/A	0.05	0	103
IBM-CM	43.95	44.08	43.70	44.20	0	13	65.00	IBM-OM	0.05	0.00	N/A	0.05	0	10
IBM-CN	38.95	39.08	38.70	39.20	0	13	70.00	IBM-ON	0.05	0.00	N/A	0.05	0	10
IBM-CO	33.90	34.08	33.70	34.10	0	0	75.00	IBM-OO	0.05	0.00	N/A	0.05	0	509
IBM-CP	29.15	29.08	28.90	29.40	0	52	80.00	IBM-OP	0.10	0.00	0.05	0.15	17	158
IBM-CQ	24.20	24.08	23.90	24.50	0	95	85.00	IBM-OQ	0.20	0.00	0.15	0.25	26	447
IBM-CR	19.20	19.08	19.10	19.40	13	183	90.00	IBM-OR	0.40	0.00	0.35	0.45	121	829
IBM-CS	14.80	14.08	14.70	14.90	2	310	95.00	IBM-OS	0.80	0.00	0.75	0.85	0	587
IBM-CT	10.45	9.08	10.30	10.60	68	801	100.00	IBM-OT	1.55	0.00	1.50	1.60	201	2,244
IBM-CA	6.80	4.08	6.70	6.90	165	719	105.00	IBM-OA	2.83	0.00	2.75	2.90	117	1,009
IBM-CB	3.75	0.00	3.70	3.80	415	1,395	110.00	IBM-OB	4.85	0.92	4.70	5.00	1,038	4,209
IBM-CC	1.77	0.00	1.70	1.85	145	2,113	115.00	IBM-OC	7.80	5.92	7.70	7.90	101	110
IBM-CD	0.68	0.00	0.60	0.75	439	1,337	120.00	IBM-OD	11.75	10.92	11.60	11.90	10	59
IBM-CE	0.20	0.00	0.15	0.25	0	167	125.00	IBM-OE	16.55	15.92	16.30	16.80	0	16
IBM-CF	0.10	0.00	N/A	0.10	0	0	130.00	IBM-OF	21.40	20.92	21.10	21.70	0	0
IBM-CG	0.05	0.00	N/A	0.05	0	0	135.00	IBM-OG	26.35	25.92	26.10	26.60	0	0
IBM-CH	0.05	0.00	N/A	0.05	0	0	140.00	IBM-OH	31.40	30.92	31.10	31.70	0	0

For color charts go to: www.traderslibrary.com/TLECorner • Chart by: thinkorswim.com

shows a current intrinsic value of $9.08. This means that if you were
to purchase the $100 call option and paid $10.60 (ask price), then
$9.08 of the $10.60 cost is equity (intrinsic value), leaving a difference of $1.52, which is called extrinsic value. Before we discuss
extrinsic value, we need to review Figure 2.6 to learn intrinsic value
for a put option.

The intrinsic value for the $115 put option is $5.92, which represents an equity value for this option. With a cost of $7.90 and an
intrinsic value of $5.92, we're left with a value of $1.98, which represents the extrinsic value.

It's important that you know that intrinsic value (equity) is the difference between your strike price and the current price of the stock.
Using the call option example, you should remember that this in-

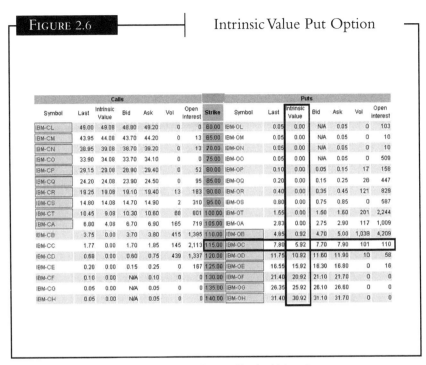

	Calls							Puts						
Symbol	Last	Intrinsic Value	Bid	Ask	Vol	Open Interest	Strike	Symbol	Last	Intrinsic Value	Bid	Ask	Vol	Open Interest
IBM-CL	49.00	49.08	48.80	49.20	0	0	60.00	IBM-OL	0.05	0.00	N/A	0.05	0	103
IBM-CM	43.95	44.08	43.70	44.20	0	13	65.00	IBM-OM	0.05	0.00	N/A	0.05	0	10
IBM-CN	38.95	39.08	38.70	39.20	0	13	70.00	IBM-ON	0.05	0.00	N/A	0.05	0	10
IBM-CO	33.90	34.08	33.70	34.10	0	0	75.00	IBM-OO	0.05	0.00	N/A	0.05	0	509
IBM-CP	29.15	29.08	28.90	29.40	0	52	80.00	IBM-OP	0.10	0.00	0.05	0.15	17	158
IBM-CQ	24.20	24.08	23.90	24.50	0	95	85.00	IBM-OQ	0.20	0.00	0.15	0.25	28	447
IBM-CR	19.25	19.08	19.10	19.40	13	183	90.00	IBM-OR	0.40	0.00	0.35	0.45	121	829
IBM-CS	14.80	14.08	14.70	14.90	2	310	95.00	IBM-OS	0.80	0.00	0.75	0.85	0	587
IBM-CT	10.45	9.08	10.30	10.60	68	801	100.00	IBM-OT	1.55	0.00	1.50	1.60	201	2,244
IBM-CA	6.80	4.08	6.70	6.90	165	719	105.00	IBM-OA	2.83	0.00	2.75	2.90	117	1,009
IBM-CB	3.75	0.00	3.70	3.80	415	1,395	110.00	IBM-OB	4.85	0.92	4.70	5.00	1,038	4,209
IBM-CC	1.77	0.00	1.70	1.85	145	2,113	115.00	IBM-OC	7.80	5.92	7.70	7.90	101	110
IBM-CD	0.68	0.00	0.60	0.75	439	1,337	120.00	IBM-OD	11.75	10.92	11.60	11.90	10	58
IBM-CE	0.20	0.00	0.15	0.25	0	167	125.00	IBM-OE	16.55	15.92	16.30	16.80	0	16
IBM-CF	0.10	0.00	N/A	0.10	0	0	130.00	IBM-OF	21.40	20.92	21.10	21.70	0	0
IBM-CG	0.05	0.00	N/A	0.05	0	0	135.00	IBM-OG	26.35	25.92	26.10	26.60	0	0
IBM-CH	0.05	0.00	N/A	0.05	0	0	140.00	IBM-OH	31.40	30.92	31.10	31.70	0	0

FIGURE 2.6 — Intrinsic Value Put Option

For color charts go to: www.traderslibrary.com/TLECorner • Chart by: thinkorswim.com

trinsic value increases with the stock and decreases when the stock drops. The reverse effect applies when looking at the put option example; as the stock value drops, your intrinsic value will increase and as the stock price increases, your intrinsic value will drop.

LINGO

Intrinsic value (or equity) is the difference between your strike price and the current price of the stock. This is the part of the cost that is actually part of the option's value.

Extrinsic value is the difference between an option's price and the intrinsic value. This is additional money you pay that you will not get back (it is not equity).

Extrinsic Value

The portion of your option that is not equity is known as extrinsic value, which is the difference between an option's price and the intrinsic value. Figure 2.7 shows the April $115 call option for IBM with an intrinsic value of $4.16 and an extrinsic value of $1.99, totaling $6.15. This would be your cost to purchase this April $115 call option based upon the bid price of $6.00 and ask price of $6.30.

Keep in mind that the lower the strike price, the greater the cost of the call option, the larger your intrinsic value, and the smaller your extrinsic value will be. Of the various parts of an option, this is the portion you must truly understand. I refer to extrinsic value as fluff or garbage, meaning this additional cost of $1.99 is an additional cost you pay when buying an option. To simplify: extrinsic value is

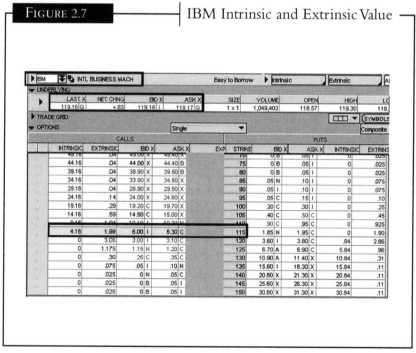

FIGURE 2.7 — IBM Intrinsic and Extrinsic Value

For color charts go to: www.traderslibrary.com/TLECorner • Chart by: thinkorswim.com

an additional cost you pay for an option that you'll never get back.

Viewed in another way, we'll use an example of Apple's iPhone. When it was first released, thousands stood in line to purchase the phone thinking the price would go higher at a later time; yet, the price actually dropped $100 a few months later. To me the hype of buying the phone created the fluff, which is what in the options market equals extrinsic value. It doesn't necessarily mean the price of the phone, or in Figure 2.8 the IBM stock, will move higher because people may be willing to buy that option over another option.

Looking at the same example, you'll notice that the extrinsic value for the lower strike prices of $110 and below have less extrinsic value. On the other hand the $120 strike price, which is the closest

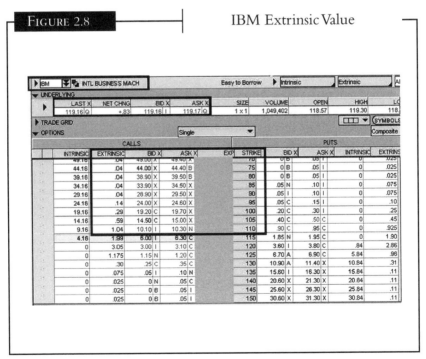

FIGURE 2.8   IBM Extrinsic Value

For color charts go to: www.traderslibrary.com/TLECorner • Chart by: thinkorswim.com

to the current price of the stock ($119.16), has the greatest extrinsic value (fluff) of $3.05. It also has a value of zero for the intrinsic side of the option, which again is the equity portion of your option's cost. When referring to the April $120 call option (Figure 2.9), your bid price is $3.00, your ask price $3.10, and your extrinsic value $3.05. In this example, the time portion of the option represents five weeks before the April expiration day.

Running the numbers, you know that if you were to purchase the $120 April call option and paid $3.05 per share ($305 per contract), then you'll need the stock price to increase from its current price of $119.16 above your strike price of $120 plus your $3.05 cost. This means your break even price will be $123.05; so, if the stock doesn't increase above $123.05, you'll lose $3.05 per share, equaling $305

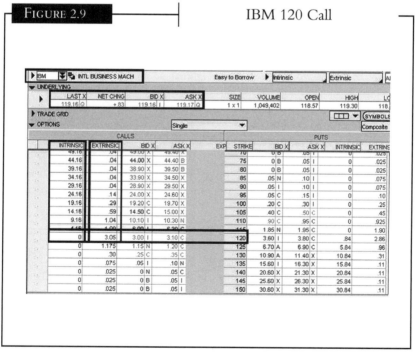

FIGURE 2.9   IBM 120 Call

BM	INTL BUSINESS MACH			Easy to Borrow	Intrinsic	Extrinsic	A
UNDERLYING							

LAST X	NET CHNG	BID X	ASK X	SIZE	VOLUME	OPEN	HIGH	LO
119.16 Q	+.83	119.16 I	119.17 Q	1 x 1	1,049,402	118.57	119.30	118.

TRADE GRID · OPTIONS · Single · SYMBOL · Composite

	CALLS						PUTS		
INTRINSIC	EXTRINSIC	BID X	ASK X	EXP	STRIKE	BID X	ASK X	INTRINSIC	EXTRINS
49.16	.04	49.00 X	49.40 X		70	0 B	.05 I	0	.025
44.16	.04	44.00 X	44.40 B		75	0 B	.05 I	0	.025
39.16	.04	38.90 X	39.50 B		80	0 B	.05 I	0	.025
34.16	.04	33.90 X	34.50 X		85	.05 N	.10 I	0	.075
29.16	.04	28.90 X	29.50 X		90	.05 I	.10 I	0	.075
24.16	.14	24.00 X	24.60 X		95	.05 C	.15 I	0	.10
19.16	.29	19.20 C	19.70 X		100	.20 C	.30 I	0	.25
14.16	.59	14.50 C	15.00 X		105	.40 C	.50 C	0	.45
9.16	1.04	10.10 I	10.30 N		110	.90 C	.95 C	0	.925
4.16	1.00	6.00 I	6.30 C		115	1.85 N	1.95 C	0	1.90
0	3.05	3.00 I	3.10 C		120	3.60 I	3.80 C	.84	2.86
0	1.175	1.15 N	1.20 C		125	6.70 A	6.90 C	5.84	.96
0	.30	.25 C	.35 C		130	10.90 A	11.40 X	10.84	.31
0	.075	.05 I	.10 N		135	15.60 I	16.30 X	15.84	.11
0	.025	0 N	.05 C		140	20.60 X	21.30 X	20.84	.11
0	.025	0 B	.05 I		145	25.60 X	26.30 X	25.84	.11
0	.025	0 B	.05 I		150	30.60 X	31.30 X	30.84	.11

For color charts go to: www.traderslibrary.com/TLECorner • Chart by: thinkorswim.com

per contract. If, however, the stock was to increase to say, a price of $125, your profit for the April 120 call option would be $1.95 per share. To determine this profit, we subtract the stock price of $125 away from your actual break even price of $123.05 for a total of $1.95, or $195 per contract (100 shares).

To determine your profit in another way, subtract your $120 strike price from the stock's current price of $125 to get a total of $5, or $500 per contract. Then, subtract your option cost of $305 per contract giving you a profit of $195 per contract.

So our lesson regarding extrinsic value is one of simplicity: you

Two Ways to Determine Profit

[Stock Price-Break Even Price] x 100 = Profit
[125 – 123.05] x 100 = $195
{[Stock Price-Strike Price] x 100} – [Option Cost] = Profit
{[125-120] x100} – 305 = $195
* Brackets mean absolute value

don't want to purchase an option that has such increased extrinsic value so the lower the extrinsic value the more you'll benefit when the stock moves higher. If you had owned the stock IBM, you would benefit from the high extrinsic value if you were to sell this 120 call option creating a covered call. You may now see why many directional call option buyers fail because the stock must move up equal to the time/extrinsic value before you break even. Let this be an eye-opening lesson. As you read on, always remember this: successful option traders sell options that have high extrinsic value instead of purchasing options with high extrinsic value.

Successful option traders sell options that have high extrinsic value instead of purchasing options with high extrinsic value.

FIGURE 2.10 — Call Option Volume

Symbol	Last	Intrinsic Value	Bid	Ask	Vol	Open Interest	Strike (Mar 08)	Symbol	Last	Intrinsic Value	Bid	Ask	Vol	Open Interest
IM-CL	49.00	49.08	48.80	49.20	0	0	60.00	IBM-OL	0.05	0.00	N/A	0.05	0	103
IM-CM	43.95	44.08	43.70	44.20	0	13	65.00	IBM-OM	0.05	0.00	N/A	0.05	0	10
IM-CN	38.95	39.08	38.70	39.20	0	13	70.00	IBM-ON	0.05	0.00	N/A	0.05	0	10
IM-CO	33.90	34.08	33.70	34.10	0	0	75.00	IBM-OO	0.05	0.00	N/A	0.05	0	509
IM-CP	29.15	29.08	28.90	29.40	0	52	80.00	IBM-OP	0.10	0.00	0.05	0.15	17	158
IM-CQ	24.20	24.08	23.90	24.50	0	95	85.00	IBM-OQ	0.20	0.00	0.15	0.25	26	447
IM-CR	19.25	19.08	19.10	19.40	13	183	90.00	IBM-OR	0.40	0.00	0.35	0.45	121	829
IM-CS	14.80	14.08	14.70	14.90	2	310	95.00	IBM-OS	0.80	0.00	0.75	0.85	0	587
IM-CT	10.45	9.08	10.30	10.60	68	801	100.00	IBM-OT	1.55	0.00	1.50	1.60	201	2,244
IM-CA	6.80	4.08	6.70	6.90	165	719	105.00	IBM-OA	2.83	0.00	2.75	2.90	117	1,009
IM-CB	3.75	0.00	3.70	3.80	415	1,395	110.00	IBM-OB	4.85	0.92	4.70	5.00	1,038	4,209
IM-CC	1.77	0.00	1.70	1.85	145	2,113	115.00	IBM-OC	7.80	5.92	7.70	7.90	101	110
IM-CD	0.68	0.00	0.60	0.75	439	1,337	120.00	IBM-OD	11.75	10.92	11.60	11.90	10	58
IM-CE	0.20	0.00	0.15	0.25	0	167	125.00	IBM-OE	16.55	15.92	16.30	16.80	0	16
IM-CF	0.10	0.00	N/A	0.10	0	0	130.00	IBM-OF	21.40	20.92	21.10	21.70	0	0
IM-CG	0.05	0.00	N/A	0.05	0	0	135.00	IBM-OG	26.35	25.92	26.10	26.60	0	0
IM-CH	0.05	0.00	N/A	0.05	0	0	140.00	IBM-OH	31.40	30.92	31.10	31.70	0	0

For color charts go to: www.traderslibrary.com/TLECorner • Chart by: thinkorswim.com

IMPORTANCE OF VOLUME

Volume is used for both stocks and options. When we reference volume for options, we're referring to how many contracts have been traded for that day. Keep in mind that an option's volume is for both the number of call options and put options that have been traded for that strike price and expiration date. Referring to Figure 2.10, you'll notice that the volume for the 90 call option had a total daily volume of 13 contracts for the month of March. If you look at the 125 strike price, the daily volume was 0, meaning that no one bought or sold the March 90 call that day.

Now looking at the same option price chart, let's look at the put options (Figure 2.11). You'll notice that the 90 March strike price has a daily volume of 121 contracts, representing the 121 contracts that have been bought and sold for the day. On the other hand, the

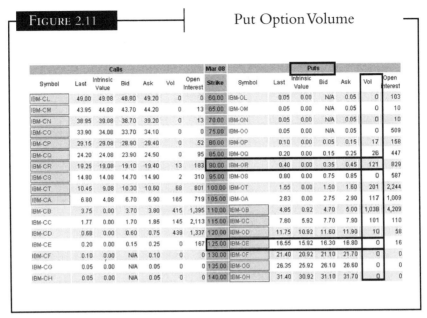

FIGURE 2.11

Put Option Volume

		Calls					Mar 08				Puts				
Symbol	Last	Intrinsic Value	Bid	Ask	Vol	Open Interest	Strike	Symbol	Last	Intrinsic Value	Bid	Ask	Vol	Open Interest
IBM-CL	49.00	49.08	48.80	49.20	0	0	60.00	IBM-OL	0.05	0.00	N/A	0.05	0	103
IBM-CM	43.95	44.08	43.70	44.20	0	13	65.00	IBM-OM	0.05	0.00	N/A	0.05	0	10
IBM-CN	38.95	39.08	38.70	39.20	0	13	70.00	IBM-ON	0.05	0.00	N/A	0.05	0	10
IBM-CO	33.90	34.08	33.70	34.10	0	0	75.00	IBM-OO	0.05	0.00	N/A	0.05	0	509
IBM-CP	29.15	29.08	28.90	29.40	0	52	80.00	IBM-OP	0.10	0.00	0.05	0.15	17	158
IBM-CQ	24.20	24.08	23.90	24.50	0	95	85.00	IBM-OQ	0.20	0.00	0.15	0.25	26	447
IBM-CR	19.25	19.08	19.10	19.40	13	183	90.00	IBM-OR	0.40	0.00	0.35	0.45	121	829
IBM-CS	14.80	14.08	14.70	14.90	2	310	95.00	IBM-OS	0.80	0.00	0.75	0.85	0	587
IBM-CT	10.45	9.08	10.30	10.60	68	801	100.00	IBM-OT	1.55	0.00	1.50	1.60	201	2,244
IBM-CA	6.80	4.08	6.70	6.90	165	719	105.00	IBM-OA	2.83	0.00	2.75	2.90	117	1,009
IBM-CB	3.75	0.00	3.70	3.80	415	1,395	110.00	IBM-OB	4.85	0.92	4.70	5.00	1,038	4,209
IBM-CC	1.77	0.00	1.70	1.85	145	2,113	115.00	IBM-OC	7.80	5.92	7.70	7.90	101	110
IBM-CD	0.68	0.00	0.60	0.75	439	1,337	120.00	IBM-OD	11.75	10.92	11.60	11.90	10	58
IBM-CE	0.20	0.00	0.15	0.25	0	167	125.00	IBM-OE	16.55	15.92	16.30	16.80	0	16
IBM-CF	0.10	0.00	N/A	0.10	0	0	130.00	IBM-OF	21.40	20.92	21.10	21.70	0	0
IBM-CG	0.05	0.00	N/A	0.05	0	0	135.00	IBM-OG	26.35	25.92	26.10	26.60	0	0
IBM-CH	0.05	0.00	N/A	0.05	0	0	140.00	IBM-OH	31.40	30.92	31.10	31.70	0	0

For color charts go to: www.traderslibrary.com/TLECorner • Chart by: thinkorswim.com

125 March put option has a daily volume of 0, representing that there were no option contracts bought or sold for the day.

Open interest is similar to volume but in this case we are actually looking at the total number of option contracts that are open for that exact option, for that exact strike price, and for that exact expiration. Looking at Figure 2.12, you'll notice that the open interest for a $90 call option is a total of 183 contracts, and the 125 call option has a total open interest of 167 contracts.

This next example shows you how to review your volume and open interest with the use of various brokerage accounts (in this case, thinkorswim.com). As you notice in this Figure 2.13, I used the drop down choices on the top right side of the trade form and selected "volume" for the first choice. Further on the right, I selected "open interest" for my second choice. Now, as you look at the chart, you'll see number one represents the call options, and number two

FIGURE 2.12 — Call Option Open Interest

Symbol	Last	Intrinsic Value	Bid	Ask	Vol	Open Interest	Strike	Symbol	Last	Intrinsic Value	Bid	Ask	Vol	Open Interest
IBM-CL	49.00	49.08	48.80	49.20		0	60.00	IBM-OL	0.05	0.00	N/A	0.05	0	103
IBM-CM	43.95	44.08	43.70	44.20		13	85.00	IBM-OM	0.05	0.00	N/A	0.05	0	10
IBM-CN	38.95	39.08	38.70	39.20		13	70.00	IBM-ON	0.05	0.00	N/A	0.05	0	10
IBM-CO	33.90	34.08	33.70	34.10		0	75.00	IBM-OO	0.05	0.00	N/A	0.05	0	509
IBM-CP	29.15	29.08	28.90	29.40		52	80.00	IBM-OP	0.10	0.00	0.05	0.15	17	158
IBM-CQ	24.20	24.08	23.90	24.50		95	85.00	IBM-OQ	0.20	0.00	0.15	0.25	26	447
IBM-CR	19.25	19.08	19.10	19.40	1	183	90.00	IBM-OR	0.40	0.00	0.35	0.45	121	829
IBM-CS	14.80	14.08	14.70	14.90		310	95.00	IBM-OS	0.80	0.00	0.75	0.85	0	587
IBM-CT	10.45	9.08	10.30	10.60	6	801	100.00	IBM-OT	1.55	0.00	1.50	1.60	201	2,244
IBM-CA	6.80	4.08	6.70	6.90	16	719	105.00	IBM-OA	2.83	0.00	2.75	2.90	117	1,009
IBM-CB	3.75	0.00	3.70	3.80	41	1,395	110.00	IBM-OB	4.85	0.92	4.70	5.00	1,038	4,209
IBM-CC	1.77	0.00	1.70	1.85	14	2,113	115.00	IBM-OC	7.80	5.92	7.70	7.90	101	110
IBM-CD	0.68	0.00	0.60	0.75	43	1,337	120.00	IBM-OD	11.75	10.92	11.60	11.90	10	58
IBM-CE	0.20	0.00	0.15	0.25		167	125.00	IBM-OE	16.55	15.92	16.30	16.80	0	16
IBM-CF	0.10	0.00	N/A	0.10		0	130.00	IBM-OF	21.40	20.92	21.10	21.70	0	0
IBM-CG	0.05	0.00	N/A	0.05		0	135.00	IBM-OG	26.35	25.92	26.10	26.60	0	0
IBM-CH	0.05	0.00	N/A	0.05		0	140.00	IBM-OH	31.40	30.92	31.10	31.70	0	0

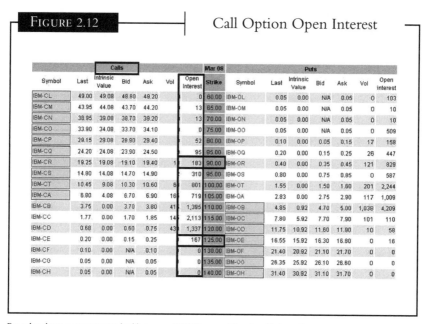

For color charts go to: www.traderslibrary.com/TLECorner • Chart by: thinkorswim.com

FIGURE 2.13 — Volume and Open Interest Settings

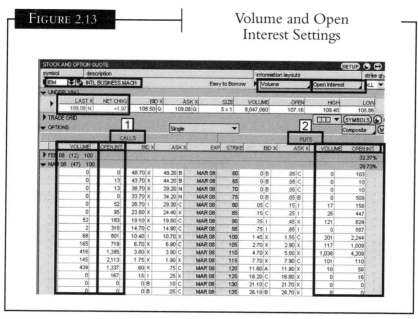

For color charts go to: www.traderslibrary.com/TLECorner • Chart by: thinkorswim.com

represents the put options. Underneath each of these, you'll see the volume and open interest for each option you're viewing.

Now that you have a good understanding of volume and open interest, let's talk about how it can be of help to you as an options trader. If you don't see any daily volume, you may create the volume as you're placing your trade, which could mean that you won't get your asking price. You may have to accept a lower price if you're selling the option and pay a higher price if you're buying an option. As for open interest, it is extremely important because it helps determine if you're interested in placing the trade or not.

Say that you were looking at an IBM 125 call option for the month of March, and you were interested in either buying or selling this option. The open interest of 167 contracts tells you that very few people have traded this option. It's not fun to be at a party alone; so, I would look for a larger party of at least 1,000 people (contracts). Keep in mind that open interest is investors both buying or selling that option, and as they continue to buy and sell until expiration date, the open interest will increase or decrease.

Knowing this, as a buyer of the stock, if the stock doesn't move above $125 per share, you'll lose your investment money. But, if the stock remained below the $125 price and you were the seller, you were profitable keeping the premium.

You'll learn to trade options with large amounts of open interest because prices have a tendency to move more if they have greater volatility, which is created by larger amounts of interest within the stock itself and the various options. Next, let's discuss implied and historical volatility of an option.

Implied Volatility and Historical Volatility

Historical volatility represents the expected volatility of a stock over the life of the option. As expectations change, option premiums react appropriately. Implied volatility is directly influenced by the supply and demand of the underlying options and by the market's expectation of the share price's direction. As expectations rise, or as the demand for an option increases, implied volatility will rise. Options that have high levels of implied volatility will result in high-priced option premiums. Conversely, as the market's expectations decrease, or demand for an option diminishes, implied volatility will decrease.

Options containing lower levels of implied volatility will result in cheaper option prices. This is important because the rise and fall of implied volatility will determine how expensive or cheap time value is to the option. The success of an options trade can be significantly enhanced by being on the right side of implied volatility changes. For example, if you own options when implied volatility increases, the price of these options climbs higher. However, a change in implied volatility for the worse can create greater losses, even when you are right about the stock's direction. Each listed option has a unique sensitivity to implied volatility changes.

For example, shorter-dated options will be less sensitive to implied volatility, while longer-dated options will be more sensitive. This is based on the fact that longer-dated options have more time value priced into them, while shorter-dated options have less time value built into them. Also, consider that each strike price will respond differently to implied volatility changes. Options with strike prices that are near-the-money are most sensitive to implied volatility changes, while options that are further in-the-money or out-of-the-money will be less sensitive to implied volatility changes. An option's sensitivity to implied volatility changes can be determined by vega—a Greek option term that tells you how much the option price can change even if the underlying stock price doesn't change. Keep in mind that as the stock's price fluctuates and as the time until expiration passes, vega values increase or decrease, depending on these changes. This means that an option can become more or less sensitive to implied volatility changes.

There are several ways to use implied volatility to your advantage, but first you need to be able to analyze it. One effective way to analyze implied volatility is to examine a chart. Many charting platforms, such as www. prophet.net, provide ways to chart an underlying option's average implied volatility, in which multiple implied volatility values are tallied up and averaged together. Figure 2.14 shows the average implied volatility of eBay, and as you'll see, I've boxed the area between 35 and 40. This indicates the range at which the option prices would be considered to be normal according to implied volatility. The area below 35 represents lower implied volatility (lower option costs), and the area above 40 represents higher implied volatility (high option costs).

CAUTION

Remember, there are many factors to consider when analyzing implied volatility. The values of implied volatility will vary depending on the type of underlying stock, the strike price, and the expiration date, which is why implied volatility must be viewed on a relative basis. Vega can help you determine how much the option will change according to the stock and the passage of time to expiration. Vega values will fluctuate meaning that options can become more or less sensitive to implied volatility changes. This sensitivity to implied volatility (low levels versus high) will also affect how expensive the option is to purchase—an important factor to consider when analyzing your risk versus reward on a trade.

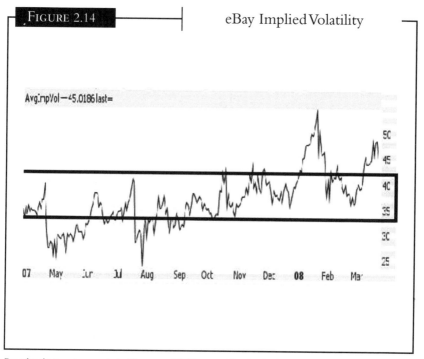

FIGURE 2.14 — eBay Implied Volatility

For color charts go to: www.traderslibrary.com/TLECorner • Chart by: thinkorswim.com

This figure shows that implied volatility fluctuates the same way prices do. Implied volatility is expressed in percentage terms and is relative to the underlying stock and how volatile it is. For example, eBay (EBAY) stock will have lower volatility values than Apple Computer (AAPL) because Apple's stock is much more volatile than eBay. Apple's volatility range will be much higher than eBay's. What might be considered a low percentage value for Apple might be considered relatively high for eBay. Because each stock has a unique implied volatility range, these values should not be compared to another stock's volatility range.

Implied volatility should be analyzed on a relative basis. In other words, after you have determined the implied volatility range for the option you are trading, you will not want to compare it against another. What is considered a relatively high value for one company

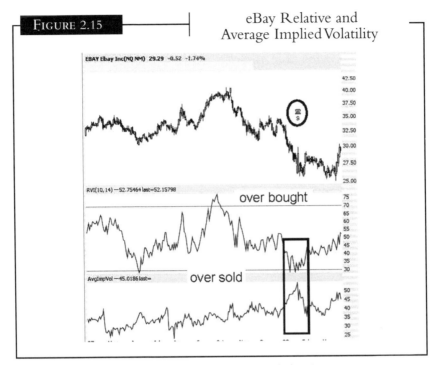

FIGURE 2.15 — eBay Relative and Average Implied Volatility

For color charts go to: www.traderslibrary.com/TLECorner • Chart by: thinkorswim.com

might be considered low for another. For example, if we were to say that eBay's normal volatility range is between 35 and 45, then Apple's normal volatility could be between 40 and 50. What you need to remember is that implied volatility of any type can affect your investment outcome because your cost of an option could be greater than what you truly should pay, which could result in greater losses even if the stock doesn't move.

Figure 2.15 illustrates the use of both relative implied volatility (RVI) and implied volatility. As you'll notice, the notes show the RVI as being oversold, yet at that time the implied volatility was at its high of over 60 (when normally it should be between 35 and 40). This is a perfect example of when not to buy any option, whether it's a call (upside potential) or put (downside potential) because the unexpected earnings news (seen within the circle and represented by the telephone and dollar sign icons) could drive the stock up or down. Why? Because the market makers over-price options to limit their risk. Knowing that options are over-priced actually helps a good investor; you'll select an investment strategy that will best fit your needs, which often will involve selling an over-priced option instead of buying.

You've probably heard that you should buy undervalued options and sell overvalued options. While this process is not as easy as it sounds, it is a great methodology to follow when selecting an appropriate option strategy. Your ability to properly evaluate and forecast implied volatility will make the process of buying cheap options and selling expensive options that much easier.

FOUR THINGS TO CONSIDER WHEN FORECASTING IMPLIED VOLATILITY

1. Make sure you can determine whether implied volatility is high or low and whether it is rising or falling. Remember, as implied volatility increases, option premiums become more expensive. As implied volatility decreases, options become less expensive. As implied volatility reaches extreme highs or lows, it is likely to revert back to its mid-price.

2. If you come across options that yield expensive premiums due to high implied volatility, understand that there is a reason. Check the news to see what caused such high company expectations and high demand for the options. It is not uncommon to see implied volatility peak ahead of earnings announcements, merger and acquisition rumors, product approvals, and other news events. Because this is when a lot of price movement takes place, the demand to participate in such events will drive option prices higher. Keep in mind that after the market-anticipated event occurs, implied volatility will collapse and revert back to its mid-price. It's

almost like taking a needle to a balloon; once the news is released, the balloon will pop with the smallest poke of the needle.

3. When you see options trading with high implied volatility levels, consider selling strategies. As option premiums become relatively expensive, they are less attractive to purchase and more desirable to sell. Such strategies include covered calls, naked puts, short straddles, and credit spreads. By contrast, there will be times when you discover relatively cheap options, such as when implied volatility is trading at or near historical lows. Many option investors use this opportunity to purchase long-dated options and look to hold them through a forecasted volatility increase.

4. When you discover options that are trading with low implied volatility levels, consider buying strategies. With relatively cheap time premiums, options are more attractive to purchase and less desirable to sell. Such strategies include buying calls, puts, debit, or credit spreads.

Now, let's use this information to talk further about the terms in-the-money, at-the-money, and out-of-the-money and why they are critical to successfully trading options.

IN-THE-MONEY CALL OPTIONS

In-the-money refers to the option strike price versus the current stock price. It is said that when your chosen strike price for a call option is lower than the current price of the stock, your option is in-the-money (ITM) because a portion of your call option investment has intrinsic value.

For example, let's say you purchased the $50 call option for stock XYZ. At the time you purchased the call option, it cost you $4.00 per share and the stock's current value was $52 per share. Your option is in-the-money by $2, which is the difference between your

---

LINGO

Intrinsic Value is the strike price of the option relative to the actual price of the underlying asset. Also known as equity.

Time Value is the length of time remaining prior to the option's expiration date.

Volatility Value describes the degree to which the price of the underlying asset fluctuates.

Option Premium equals Intrinsic Value + Time Value + Volatility Value

---

strike price ($50) and the current price of the stock, $52. Again, this is known as an in-the-money option because your strike price is lower than the stock's current price by $2, which means you have the right to buy the stock at $50 even if it trades at $52 or any price higher.

Remember, when you purchase a call option, you have the right, not the obligation, to buy the stock at a set price known as the strike price on or before a certain date, know as the expiration date. If you're thinking that successful investors purchase call options in order to have the right to buy the stock, you're not thinking like a true leverage investor. As the stock increases in value, your option will increase in value and, with the push of a button, you can sell that option for the current value.

Let's say that the $50 call option you purchased at $4 per share increases to a value of $6 per share. You can then sell that option at the current bid price and give up your right to buy the stock and walk away with a profit of $2 per share, or 50% return on your investment. Now that is leverage—you only needed $400 (one contract) cash in your brokerage account versus $5,000 for 100 shares of the stock, and worse case scenario, you cannot lose any more

FIGURE 2.16 — ITM Call Option

		Calls				Stock price $158.80		Puts				
Symbol	Last	Intrinsic Value	Bid	Ask	Vol	Open Interest	Strike	Symbol	Last	Intrinsic Value	Bid	Ask	Vol	Open Interest
QAA-BT	58.88	58.80	58.65	59.10	108	173	100.00	QAA-NT	0.28	0.00	0.26	3.30	1 241	1 306
QAA-BA	54.08	53.80	53.85	54.30	71	164	105.00	QAA-NA	0.41	0.00	0.38	3.43	1 322	896
QAA-BB	49.62	48.80	49.50	49.75	148	155	110.00	QAA-NB	0.58	0.00	0.54	3.63	673	851
QAA-BC	44.52	43.80	44.40	44.65	150	216	115.00	QAA-NC	0.87	0.00	0.85	3.89	1 524	801
QAA-BD	40.12	38.80	40.00	40.25	280	243	120.00	QAA-ND	1.21	0.00	1.17	1.25	2 361	1 338
APV-BE	35.67	33.80	35.60	35.75	412	339	125.00	APV-NE	1.77	0.00	1.74	1.80	1 291	2 181
APV-BF	30.95	28.80	30.85	31.05	1,085	450	130.00	APV-NF	2.52	0.00	2.50	2.55	2 073	3 313
APV-BG	27.07	23.80	26.95	27.20	924	641	135.00	APV-NG	3.20	0.00	3.10	3.30	2 085	7 961
APV-BH	23.45	18.80	23.40	23.50	1,787	3,101	140.00	APV-NH	4.32	0.00	4.30	4.35	5 309	7 290
APV-B	19.38	13.80	19.35	19.40	1,556	1,416	145.00	APV-NI	5.68	0.00	5.65	5.70	5 585	10 018
APV-BJ	16.23	8.80	16.20	16.30	4,463	3,111	151.00	APV-NJ	7.28	0.00	7.25	7.30	7 828	8 953
APV-BK	13.50	3.80	13.45	13.55	7,924	6,313	155.00	APV-NK	9.82	0.00	9.80	3.85	6 902	8 056
AFV-BL	10.28	0.00	10.25		17,221	18,088	160.00	APV-NL	11.80	1.20	11.75	11.85	5 583	16 976
AFV-BM	8.43	0.00	8.40	8.45	7,807	9,501	165.00	APV-NM	14.62	6.20	14.60	14.65	3 805	15 829
AFV-BN	6.32	0.00	6.30	6.35	8,971	18,712	170.00	APV-NN	17.70	11.20	17.65	17.75	2 341	11 716
AFV-BO	5.03	0.00	5.00	5.05	10,134	15,984	175.00	APV-NO	20.88	16.20	20.80	23.95	1 080	11 279
AFV-BP	3.70	0.00	3.65	3.75	9,473	20,224	180.00	APV-NP	24.92	21.20	24.90	24.95	2 713	10 978
AFV-BQ	2.73	0.00	2.71	2.74	4,955	14,650	185.00	APV-NQ	29.23	26.20	29.15	23.30	90	10 494
AFV-BR	1.98	0.00	1.95	2.00	5,742	15,417	190.00	APV-NR	33.65	31.20	33.55	33.75	213	5 277

For color charts go to: www.traderslibrary.com/TLECorner • Chart by: thinkorswim.com

than the $400. It's not just an opportunity to increase your rate of return but also 1) having less money in a trade, 2) having more cash available for other trades, and 3) if you're wrong and the stock goes down, not losing more than the cost of the call option ($400 for this example).

With other advanced option strategies, you could lose more than your original investment but not when you purchase call or put options.

Let's look at the option chart (Figure 2.16) and view which options, both for the call and put side, are in-the-money. Beginning with the call side of the chart, you'll see the boxed area with the heading "Intrinsic Value," which presents exactly how much of your option premium for each strike price is in-the-money. To keep it simple, let's say the stock is trading at $158.80 and you purchase the $155 (call) strike price for the cost of $13.55. This would put you in-the-money by an amount of $3.80, which is the number seen within the intrinsic value column. Keep in mind that you'll need the stock to increase a minimum of $13.55 to reach a break even point for this trade. The further above this price, the more profit potential you gain, giving you the ability to have un-limited profit.

AT-THE-MONEY CALL OPTIONS

At-the-money (ATM) means the current price of the stock and your chosen strike price are the exact same or very close to each other. For example, let's say you purchase a call option (bullish) with a strike price of $50 and the current price of the stock is about $50.20 per share; we refer to this as an "at-the-money" option because the strike price of $50 and stock price of $50.20 are very close to each other. You should know that these options are often over-priced; you would be better choosing an option that is in-the-money, or sometimes, an option that is out-of-the-money.

Looking at the call option chart while the stock price is $158.80, you'll notice that the $160 call option is trading at a price of $10.30 (ask price) and the intrinsic value column shows a value of $0; this means that your cost of $10.30 is strictly for time premium and has no equity value (Figure 2.17).

FIGURE 2.17 — ATM Call Option

		Calls						Stock price $158.80	Puts					
Symbol	Last	Intrinsic Value	Bid	Ask	Vol	Open Interest	Strike	Symbol	Last	Intrinsic Value	Bid	Ask	Vol	Open Interest
QAA-BT	58.88	58.80	58.65	59.10	108	175	100.00	QAA-NT	0.28	0.00	0.26	0.30	1 241	1 306
QAA-BA	54.08	53.80	53.85	54.30	71	164	105.00	QAA-NA	0.41	0.00	0.38	0.43	1 322	696
QAA-BB	49.62	48.80	49.50	49.75	146	153	110.00	QAA-NB	0.59	0.00	0.54	0.63	673	851
QAA-BC	44.52	43.80	44.40	44.65	150	216	115.00	QAA-NC	0.87	0.00	0.85	0.89	1 524	801
QAA-BD	40.12	38.80	40.00	40.25	280	243	120.00	QAA-ND	1.21	0.00	1.17	1.25	2 361	1 338
APV-BE	35.67	33.80	35.60	35.75	412	339	125.00	APV-NE	1.77	0.00	1.74	1.80	1 291	2 181
APV-BF	30.95	28.80	30.85	31.05	1,085	450	130.00	APV-NF	2.52	0.00	2.50	2.55	2 073	3 313
APV-BG	27.07	23.80	26.95	27.20	924	641	135.00	APV-NG	3.20	0.00	3.10	3.30	2 085	7 961
APV-BH	23.45	18.80	23.40	23.50	1,787	3,101	140.00	APV-NH	4.32	0.00	4.30	4.35	5 309	7 290
APV-B	19.38	13.80	19.35	19.40	1,556	1,416	145.00	APV-NI	5.68	0.00	5.65	5.70	5 585	10 018
APV-BJ	16.23	8.80	16.20	16.25	4,463	3,111	150.00	APV-NJ	7.28	0.00	7.25	7.30	7 828	8 953
APV-BK	13.50	3.80	13.45	13.75	7,924	6,313	155.00	APV-NK	9.82	0.00	9.80	9.85	6 902	8 056
AFV-BL	10.28	0.00	10.25	10.30	7,221	18,080	160.00	APV-NL	11.80	1.20	11.75	11.85	5 583	16 976
AFV-BM	8.43	0.00	8.40	8.45	7,807	9,501	165.00	APV-NM	14.62	6.20	14.60	14.65	3 805	15 829
AFV-BN	6.32	0.00	6.30	6.35	8,971	18,712	170.00	APV-NN	17.70	11.20	17.65	17.75	2 341	11 716
AFV-BO	5.03	0.00	5.00	5.05	10,134	15,984	175.00	APV-NO	20.88	16.20	20.80	20.95	1 080	11 279
AFV-BP	3.70	0.00	3.65	3.75	9,473	20,224	180.00	APV-NP	24.92	21.20	24.90	24.95	2 713	10 978
AFV-BQ	2.73	0.00	2.71	2.74	4,955	14,650	185.00	APV-NQ	29.23	26.20	29.15	29.30	90	10 494
AFV-BR	1.98	0.00	1.95	2.00	5,742	15,417	190.00	APV-NR	33.85	31.20	33.55	33.75	213	5 277

For color charts go to: www.traderslibrary.com/TLECorner • Chart by: thinkorswim.com

OUT-OF-THE-MONEY CALL OPTIONS

We've talked about the two portions that make up an option's price (intrinsic and time value); now let's look at an example of an out-of-the-money option. For a call, an out-of-the-money (OTM) option is when the chosen strike price is higher than the current price of the stock. When referring to put options, the strike price is lower than the current price of stock. For example, XYZ stock is trading at $50 per share and you choose a call option with a $55 strike price and pay $2 for the call option. This gives you the right to purchase the stock at the strike price of $55. The stock must then move up from $50 to $55 per share plus another $2 in order to cover the cost of the call option premium, which brings the break even price to $57.

As you can imagine, your odds of success when purchasing out-of-the-money call options is very small, yet many uneducated investors will choose an out-of-the-money option because they cost less than an at-the-money or in-the-money option. Let's look at a call option chart for an out-of-the-money call option using a current stock price of $158.80 (Figure 2.18)

As you'll notice within this example, all of the out-of-the-money call option strike prices are higher than the current price of the stock ($158.80). Look at the intrinsic value for the strike prices 165 through 190; you'll see a value of zero, meaning that the cost of the option is all time premium and no equity. Actually, the $160 strike is out-of-the-money too, but because it is the closest strike price to the $158.80 stock price, many refer to that strike price as an at-the-money option.

FIGURE 2.18							OTM Call Option						

	Calls						Stock price $158.80		Puts					
Symbol	Last	Intrinsic Value	Bid	Ask	Vol	Open Interest	Strike	Symbol	Last	Intrinsic Value	Bid	Ask	Vol	Open Interest
QAA-BT	58.88	58.80	58.65	59.10	108	173	100.00	QAA-NT	0.28	0.00	0.26	0.30	1 241	1 306
QAA-BA	54.08	53.80	53.85	54.30	71	164	105.00	QAA-NA	0.41	0.00	0.38	0.43	1 322	696
QAA-BB	49.62	48.80	49.50	49.75	148	153	110.00	QAA-NB	0.58	0.00	0.54	0.63	673	851
QAA-BC	44.52	43.80	44.40	44.65	150	216	115.00	QAA-NC	0.87	0.00	0.85	0.89	1 524	801
QAA-BD	40.12	38.80	40.00	40.25	280	243	120.00	QAA-ND	1.21	0.00	1.17	1.25	2 361	1 338
APV-BE	35.67	33.80	35.60	35.75	412	339	125.00	APV-NE	1.77	0.00	1.74	1.80	1 291	2 181
APV-BF	30.95	28.80	30.85	31.05	1,085	450	130.00	APV-NF	2.52	0.00	2.50	2.55	2 073	3 313
APV-BG	27.07	23.80	26.95	27.20	924	641	135.00	APV-NG	3.20	0.00	3.10	3.30	2 085	7 961
APV-BH	23.45	18.80	23.40	23.50	1,787	3,101	140.00	APV-NH	4.32	0.00	4.30	4.35	5 309	7 290
APV-BI	19.38	13.80	19.35	19.40	1,558	1,418	145.00	APV-NI	5.68	0.00	5.65	5.70	5 585	10 018
APV-BJ	16.23	8.80	16.20	16.25	4,463	3,111	150.00	APV-NJ	7.28	0.00	7.25	7.30	7 828	8 953
APV-BK	13.50	3.80	13.45	13.55	7,924	6,313	155.00	APV-NK	9.82	0.00	9.80	9.85	6 902	8 056
AFV-BL	10.28	0.00	10.25	10.30	17,221	18,086	160.00	APV-NL	11.80	1.20	11.75	11.85	5 583	16 976
AFV-BM	8.43	0.00	8.40	8.45	7,807	9,501	165.00	APV-NM	14.62	6.20	14.60	14.65	3 805	15 829
AFV-BN	6.32	0.00	6.30	6.35	8,971	18,712	170.00	APV-NN	17.70	11.20	17.65	17.75	2 341	11 718
AFV-BO	5.03	0.00	5.00	5.05	10,134	15,984	175.00	APV-NO	20.88	16.20	20.80	20.95	1 080	11 279
AFV-BP	3.70	0.00	3.65	3.75	9,473	20,224	180.00	APV-NP	24.92	21.20	24.90	24.95	2 713	10 978
AFV-BQ	2.73	0.00	2.71	2.74	4,955	14,860	185.00	APV-NQ	29.23	26.20	29.15	23.30	90	10 494
AFV-BR	.98	0.00	1.95	2.00	5,742	15,417	190.00	APV-NR	33.65	31.20	33.55	33.75	213	5 277

For color charts go to: www.traderslibrary.com/TLECorner • Chart by: thinkorswim.com

If you purchase a call option with an out-of-the-money strike price, then you'll need the stock price to move up at least the amount you paid for the option. For example, say you selected a call option with a strike price of $165 and the cost (seen in Figure 2.19) is an ask price of $8.45. The stock price must move from its current price of $158.80 plus the amount of your option price, $8.45, for a total of $167.25 to break even. Any price below the $167.25 will mean your option will expire worthless, and you'll lose $845 for one contract (options only trade in groups of 100 shares).

I'm going to share with you how the same terms "in-the-money", "at-the-money", and "out-of-the-money" work when trading the market to the downside and using the purchase of put options to benefit as stocks drop in value. The concept is the same as call options except the visual is opposite; when the actual price of the

---

FIGURE 2.19 ———|——— OTM 165 Call Option ———

		Calls				Stock price $158.80			Puts				
Symbol	Last	Intrinsic Value	Bid	Ask	Vol	Open Interest	Strike	Symbol	Last	Intrinsic Value	Bid	Ask	Vol	Open Interest
QAA-BT	58.88	58.80	58.85	59.10	108	173	100.00	QAA-NT	0.28	0.00	0.26	0.30	1 241	1 306
QAA-BA	54.08	53.80	53.85	54.30	71	164	105.00	QAA-NA	0.41	0.00	0.38	0.43	1 322	696
QAA-BB	49.62	48.80	49.50	49.75	148	153	110.00	QAA-NB	0.58	0.00	0.54	0.63	673	851
QAA-BC	44.52	43.80	44.40	44.65	150	218	115.00	QAA-NC	0.87	0.00	0.85	0.89	1 524	801
QAA-BD	40.12	38.80	40.00	40.25	280	243	120.00	QAA-ND	1.21	0.00	1.17	1.25	2 361	1 338
APV-BE	35.67	33.80	35.60	35.75	412	338	125.00	APV-NE	1.77	0.00	1.74	1.80	1 291	2 181
APV-BF	30.95	28.80	30.85	31.05	1,085	450	130.00	APV-NF	2.52	0.00	2.50	2.55	2 073	3 313
APV-BG	27.07	23.80	26.95	27.20	924	641	135.00	APV-NG	3.20	0.00	3.10	3.30	2 085	7 961
APV-BH	23.45	18.80	23.40	23.50	1,787	3,101	140.00	APV-NH	4.32	0.00	4.30	4.35	5 309	7 290
APV-BI	19.38	13.80	19.35	19.40	1,558	1,418	145.00	APV-NI	5.68	0.00	5.65	5.70	5 585	10 018
APV-BJ	16.23	8.80	16.20	16.25	4,463	3,111	150.00	APV-NJ	7.28	0.00	7.25	7.30	7 828	8 953
APV-BK	13.50	3.80	13.45	13.55	7,924	6,313	155.00	APV-NK	9.82	0.00	9.80	9.85	6 902	8 056
AFV-BL	10.28	0.00	10.25	10.30	17,221	18,088	160.00	APV-NL	11.80	1.20	11.75	11.85	5 583	16 976
AFV-BM	8.43	0.00	8.40	8.45	7,807	9,501	165.00	APV-NM	14.62	6.20	14.60	14.65	3 805	15 829
AFV-BN	6.32	0.00	6.30	6.35	8,971	18,712	170.00	APV-NN	17.70	11.20	17.65	17.75	2 341	11 716
AFV-BO	5.03	0.00	5.00	5.05	10,134	15,984	175.00	APV-NO	20.88	16.20	20.80	20.95	1 080	11 279
AFV-BP	3.70	0.00	3.65	3.75	9,473	20,224	180.00	APV-NP	24.92	21.20	24.90	24.95	2 713	10 978
AFV-BQ	2.73	0.00	2.71	2.74	4,955	14,650	185.00	APV-NQ	29.23	26.20	29.15	29.30	90	10 494
AFV-BR	1.98	0.00	1.95	2.00	5,742	15,417	190.00	APV-NR	33.65	31.20	33.55	33.75	213	5 277

For color charts go to: www.traderslibrary.com/TLECorner • Chart by: thinkorswim.com

FIGURE 2.20		ITM Put Option

		Calls				Stock price $158.80				Puts			
Symbol	Last	Intrinsic Value	Bid	Ask	Vol	Open Interest	Strike	Symbol	Last	Intrinsic Value	Bid	Ask	Vol	Open interest
QAA-BT	58.88	58.80	58.85	59.10	108	172	100.00	QAA-NT	0.28	0.00	0.26	0.30	1 241	1 306
QAA-BA	54.08	53.80	53.85	54.30	71	164	105.00	QAA-NA	0.41	0.00	0.38	0.43	1 322	696
QAA-BB	49.62	48.80	49.50	49.75	148	153	110.00	QAA-NB	0.58	0.00	0.54	0.63	673	851
QAA-BC	44.52	43.80	44.40	44.65	150	218	115.00	QAA-NC	0.87	0.00	0.85	0.89	1 524	801
QAA-BD	40.12	38.80	40.00	40.25	280	243	120.00	QAA-ND	1.21	0.00	1.17	1.25	2 361	1 338
APV-BE	35.67	33.80	35.60	35.75	412	339	125.00	APV-NE	1.77	0.00	1.74	1.80	1 291	2 181
APV-BF	30.95	28.80	30.85	31.05	1,085	450	130.00	APV-NF	2.52	0.00	2.50	2.55	2 073	3 313
APV-BG	27.07	23.80	26.95	27.20	924	641	135.00	APV-NO	3.20	0.00	3.10	3.30	2 085	7 961
APV-BH	23.45	18.80	23.40	23.50	1,787	3,101	140.00	APV-NH	4.32	0.00	4.30	4.35	5 309	7 290
APV-BI	19.38	13.80	19.35	19.40	1,558	1,418	145.00	APV-NI	5.68	0.00	5.65	5.70	5 585	10 018
APV-BJ	16.23	8.80	16.20	16.25	4,463	3,111	150.00	APV-NJ	7.28	0.00	7.25	7.30	7 828	8 953
APV-BK	13.50	3.80	13.45	13.55	7,924	6,313	155.00	APV-NK	9.82	0.00	9.80	3.85	6 902	8 058
AFV-BL	10.28	0.00	10.25	10.30	17,221	18,086	160.00	APV-NL	11.80	1.20	11.75	11.85	5 583	16 976
AFV-BM	8.43	0.00	8.40	8.45	7,807	9,501	165.00	APV-NM	14.62	6.20	14.60	14.65	3 805	15 829
AFV-BN	6.32	0.00	6.30	6.35	8,971	18,712	170.00	APV-NN	17.70	11.20	17.85	17.75	2 341	11 716
AFV-BO	5.03	0.00	5.00	5.05	10,134	15,984	175.00	APV-NO	20.88	16.20	20.80	23.95	1 080	11 279
AFV-BP	3.70	0.00	3.65	3.75	9,473	20,224	180.00	APV-NP	24.92	21.20	24.90	24.95	2 713	10 978
AFV-BQ	2.73	0.00	2.71	2.74	4,955	14,650	185.00	APV-NQ	29.23	26.20	29.15	23.30	90	10 494
AFV-BR	1.98	0.00	1.95	2.00	5,742	15,417	190.00	APV-NR	33.65	31.20	33.55	33.75	213	5 277

For color charts go to: www.traderslibrary.com/TLECorner • Chart by: thinkorswim.com

stock is below your chosen strike price for a put option, your option is in-the-money instead of out-of-the-money.

IN-THE-MONEY PUT OPTIONS

Let's take a look at Figure 2.20. If you focus on the right side of the chart, you'll see that the first in-the-money put option will be the 160 strike price and every strike price above the $158 current price of the stock is in-the-money.

Once again the intrinsic value is what determines if an option is in-the-money. If the stock didn't move down (put option), then you could lose all but the intrinsic value. With the $165 put option, your intrinsic value is $14.65; so, if the stock remains at the current price of $158.80 come expiration and your cost for the $165 put option was

FIGURE 2.21 | ITM 165 Put Option

	Calls						Stock price $158.80		Puts				
Symbol	Last	Intrinsic Value	Bid	Ask	Vol	Open Interest	Strike	Symbol	Last	Intrinsic Value	Bid	Ask	Vol	Open Interest
QAA-BT	58.88	58.80	58.85	59.10	106	173	100.00	QAA-NT	0.28	0.00	0.26	0.30	1 241	1 306
QAA-BA	54.08	53.80	53.85	54.30	71	184	105.00	QAA-NA	0.41	0.00	0.38	0.43	1 322	696
QAA-BB	49.62	48.80	49.50	49.75	146	153	110.00	QAA-NB	0.58	0.00	0.54	0.63	673	851
QAA-BC	44.52	43.80	44.40	44.65	150	218	115.00	QAA-NC	0.87	0.00	0.85	0.89	1 524	801
QAA-BD	40.12	38.80	40.00	40.25	280	243	120.00	QAA-ND	1.21	0.00	1.17	1.25	2 361	1 338
APV-BE	35.67	33.80	35.60	35.75	412	336	125.00	APV-NE	1.77	0.00	1.74	1.80	1 291	2 181
APV-BF	30.95	28.80	30.85	31.05	1,085	450	130.00	APV-NF	2.52	0.00	2.50	2.55	2 073	3 313
APV-B3	27.07	23.80	26.95	27.20	924	641	135.00	APV-NG	3.20	0.00	3.10	3.30	2 085	7 961
APV-BH	23.45	18.80	23.40	23.50	1,787	3,101	140.00	APV-NH	4.32	0.00	4.30	4.35	5 309	7 290
APV-B	19.38	13.80	19.35	19.40	1,556	1,416	145.00	APV-NI	5.68	0.00	5.65	5.70	5 585	10 018
APV-BJ	16.23	8.80	16.20	16.25	4,463	3,111	150.00	APV-NJ	7.28	0.00	7.25	7.30	7 828	8 953
APV-BK	13.50	3.80	13.45	13.55	7,924	6,313	155.00	APV-NK	9.82	0.00	9.80	9.85	6 902	8 056
AFV-BL	10.28	0.00	10.25	10.30	17,221	18,086	160.00	APV-NL	11.80	1.20	11.75	11.85	5 583	16 976
AFV-BM	8.43	0.00	8.40	8.45	7,807	9,501	165.00	APV-NM	14.62	6.20	14.60	14.65	3 805	15 829
AFV-BN	6.32	0.00	6.30	6.35	8,971	18,712	170.00	APV-NN	17.70	11.20	17.65	17.75	2 341	11 716
AFV-BO	5.03	0.00	5.00	5.05	10,134	15,984	175.00	APV-NO	20.88	16.20	20.80	20.95	1 080	11 279
AFV-BP	3.70	0.00	3.65	3.75	9,473	20,224	180.00	APV-NP	24.92	21.20	24.90	24.95	2 713	10 978
AFV-BQ	2.73	0.00	2.71	2.74	4,955	14,650	185.00	APV-NQ	29.23	26.20	29.15	29.30	90	10 494
AFV-BR	1.98	0.00	1.95	2.00	5,742	15,417	190.00	APV-NR	33.65	31.20	33.55	33.75	213	5 277

For color charts go to: www.traderslibrary.com/TLECorner • Chart by: thinkorswim.com

$14.65 (ask price), then your loss would be $8.45 per share, or $845 for one contract. As seen in Figure 2.21, your intrinsic value (equity) is $6.20. We'll break down the details, along with your best case and worst case scenarios, when we cover the purchase of put options.

AT-THE-MONEY PUT OPTIONS

With any option, whether a call or put, the term at-the-money refers to your selected strike price being the closest to the current price of the stock. When looking at a put option (Figure 2.22) and knowing the current price of the stock is $158.80, we would say that an at-the-money option would be the $160 strike price, which has a cost of $11.85 (ask price). Although we do show an intrinsic value of $1.20, this is referred to as an at-the-money strike price

| FIGURE 2.22 | | | | | | | ATM Put Option | | | | | |

	Calls					Stock price $158.80			**Puts**			
Symbol	Last	Intrinsic Value	Bid	Ask	Vol	Open Interest	Strike	Symbol	Last	Intrinsic Value	Bid	Ask	Vol	Open Interest
QAA-BT	58.88	58.80	58.65	59.10	108	173	100.00	QAA-NT	0.28	0.00	0.26	0.30	1 241	1 306
QAA-BA	54.08	53.80	53.85	54.30	71	184	105.00	QAA-NA	0.41	0.00	0.38	0.43	1 322	696
QAA-BB	49.62	48.80	49.50	49.75	148	153	110.00	QAA-NB	0.58	0.00	0.54	0.63	673	851
QAA-BC	44.52	43.80	44.40	44.65	150	218	115.00	QAA-NC	0.87	0.00	0.85	0.89	1 524	801
QAA-BD	40.12	39.80	40.00	40.25	280	243	120.00	QAA-ND	1.21	0.00	1.17	1.25	2 361	1 338
APV-BE	35.67	33.80	35.60	35.75	412	339	125.00	APV-NE	1.77	0.00	1.74	1.80	1 291	2 181
APV-BF	30.95	28.80	30.85	31.05	1,085	450	130.00	APV-NF	2.52	0.00	2.50	2.55	2 073	3 313
APV-BG	27.07	23.80	26.95	27.20	924	641	135.00	APV-NG	3.20	0.00	3.10	3.30	2 085	7 961
APV-BH	23.45	18.80	23.40	23.50	1,787	3,101	140.00	APV-NH	4.32	0.00	4.30	4.35	5 309	7 290
APV-B	19.38	13.80	19.35	19.40	1,558	1,416	145.00	APV-NI	5.68	0.00	5.65	5.70	5 585	10 018
APV-BJ	16.23	8.80	16.20	16.25	4,463	3,111	150.00	APV-NJ	7.28	0.00	7.25	7.30	7 828	8 953
APV-BK	13.50	3.80	13.45	13.55	7,924	6,313	155.00	APV-NK	9.82	0.00	9.80	9.85	6 902	8 056
AFV-BL	10.28	0.00	10.25	10.30	17,221	18,086	160.00	APV-NL	11.80	1.20	11.75	11.85	5 583	16 976
AFV-BM	8.43	0.00	8.40	8.45	7,807	9,501	165.00	APV-NM	14.62	6.20	14.60	14.65	3 806	15 629
AFV-BN	6.32	0.00	6.30	6.35	8,971	18,712	170.00	APV-NN	17.70	11.20	17.65	17.75	2 341	11 716
AFV-BO	5.03	0.00	5.00	5.05	10,134	15,984	175.00	APV-NO	20.88	16.20	20.80	20.95	1 080	11 279
AFV-BP	3.70	0.00	3.65	3.75	9,473	20,224	180.00	APV-NP	24.92	21.20	24.90	24.95	2 713	10 978
AFV-BQ	2.73	0.00	2.71	2.74	4,955	14,650	185.00	APV-NQ	29.23	26.20	29.15	29.30	90	10 494
AFV-BR	1.98	0.00	1.95	2.00	5,742	15,417	190.00	APV-NR	33.65	31.20	33.55	33.75	213	5 277

For color charts go to: www.traderslibrary.com/TLECorner • Chart by: thinkorswim.com

because it is the closest strike price to the current price of the stock at that time.

If you're going to successfully trade put options, you would not want to purchase an at-the-money option because the cost is greater and it has more implied volatility (additional cost for no good reason) added to the price. You'll learn later that we prefer to sell options that are over-priced and not purchase them. Buying over-priced options often comes back to bite you.

OUT-OF-THE-MONEY PUT OPTIONS

Figure 2.23 shows the 110 through 155 strike prices as out-of-the-money because the current price of the stock is $158.80, which is

FIGURE 2.23 | OTM Put Options 110 through 155

	Calls						Stock price $158.80		Puts					
Symbol	Last	Intrinsic Value	Bd	Ask	Vol	Open Interest	Strike	Symbol	Last	Intrinsic Value	Bd	Ask	Vol	Open Interest
QAA-BT	58.88	58.80	58.65	59.10	10E	173	103.00	QAA-NT	0.26	0.00	0.26	0.30	1 241	1 306
QAA-BA	54.08	53.80	53.85	54.30	71	164	105.00	QAA-NA	0.41	0.00	0.38	0.43	1 322	696
QAA-BB	49.62	48.80	49.50	49.75	14E	153	110.00	QAA-NB	0.58	0.00	0.54	0.63	673	851
QAA-BC	44.52	43.80	44.40	44.65	15C	216	115.00	QAA-NC	0.87	0.00	0.85	0.89	1 524	801
QAA-BD	40.12	38.80	40.00	40.25	28C	243	120.00	QAA-ND	1.21	0.00	1.17	1.25	2 361	1 338
APV-BE	35.67	33.80	35.60	35.75	412	339	125.00	APV-NE	1.71	0.00	1.74	1.80	1 291	2 181
APV-BF	30.95	28.80	30.85	31.05	1,085	45C	130.00	APV-NF	2.51	0.00	2.50	2.55	2 073	3 313
APV-BG	27.07	23.80	26.95	27.20	924	641	135.00	APV-NG	3.20	0.00	3.10	3.30	2 085	7 961
APV-BH	23.45	18.80	23.40	23.50	1,787	3,101	140.00	APV-NH	4.32	0.00	4.30	4.35	5 309	7 290
APV-B	19.38	13.80	19.35	19.40	1,55E	1,41E	145.00	APV-NI	5.68	0.00	5.65	5.70	5 585	10 018
APV-BJ	16.23	8.80	16.20	16.25	4,48?	3,111	150.00	APV-NJ	7.2?	0.00	7.25	7.30	7 828	8 953
APV-BK	13.50	3.80	13.45	13.55	7,924	6,31?	155.00	APV-NK	9.8?	0.00	9.80	3.85	6 902	8 056
AFV-BL	10.28	0.00	10.25	10.30	17,221	18,08E	160.00	APV-NL	11.80	1.20	11.75	11.85	5 583	16 976
AFV-BM	8.43	0.00	8.40	8.45	7,807	9,501	165.00	APV-NM	14.62	6.20	14.60	14.65	3 805	15 829
AFV-BN	6.32	0.00	6.30	6.35	8,971	18,712	170.00	APV-NN	17.70	11.20	17.65	17.75	2 341	11 716
AFV-BO	5.03	0.00	5.00	5.05	10,134	15,984	175.00	APV-NO	20.88	16.20	20.80	20.95	1 080	11 279
AFV-BP	3.70	0.00	3.65	3.75	9,473	20,224	180.00	APV-NP	24.92	21.20	24.90	24.95	2 713	10 978
AFV-BQ	2.73	0.00	2.71	2.74	4,955	14,65C	185.00	APV-NQ	29.23	26.20	29.15	29.30	90	10 494
AFV-BR	.98	0.00	1.95	2.00	5,742	15,417	190.00	APV-NR	33.65	31.20	33.55	33.75	213	5 277

For color charts go to: www.traderslibrary.com/TLECorner • Chart by: thinkorswim.com

higher than these strike prices. They will only become in-the-money options when the stock price drops below these strike prices. As you'll notice, these options are less expensive than the others, which can also mean they are higher risk. If the stock doesn't go down, then your option will expire worthless and the entire cost of your put option will be a loss.

A put option can be an investment with limited risk, allowing you to make money as your underlying investment drops in value (we'll cover this in more detail in chapter six).

INSIDER SECRET

Professional option traders prefer to sell options that are over-priced. Keep this in mind when you look at ATM call and put options as these tend to have a greater cost and more implied volatility.

Purchasing Call Options

In-the-Money: strike price is lower than the current price of the stock

At-the-Money: strike price is the same or the closest to the current price of the stock

Out-of-the-Money: strike price is higher than the current price of the stock

Purchasing Put Options

In-the-Money: strike price is higher than the current price of the stock

At-the-Money: strike price is the same or the closest to the current price of the stock

Out-of-the-Money: strike price is lower than the current price of the stock

Put Option Potential–
A Sneak Peek

To get you excited about chapter six, let's look at an example of a put option on a stock that dropped. As you'll see within Figure 2.24. As you'll see within Figure 2.24. As you'll see within Figure 2.24, the company Garmin (GRMN) had a large move down and the put option price increased. Looking at the stock chart you will notice several times when the stock showed downward potential; but, the most recent drop (circled) takes the stock below $100 per share before continuing down to the price of $55.

Now if you'll look at Figure 2.25, you'll see that the cost of an April $100 put option (which is in-the-money) cost $12.30 per share, or $1,230 per contract. The put option increased to $57.05 per share ($5,705 per contract) as the stock dropped slightly more than $50

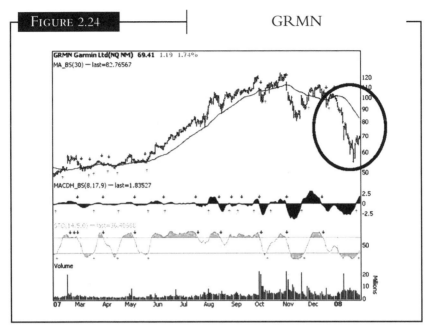

For color charts go to: www.traderslibrary.com/TLECorner • Chart by: thinkorswim.com

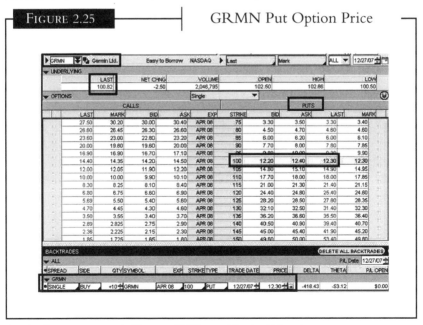

For color charts go to: www.traderslibrary.com/TLECorner • Chart by: thinkorswim.com

per share, giving us a $4,475 profit equaling a 364% rate of return for 3 ½ months (Figure 2.26).

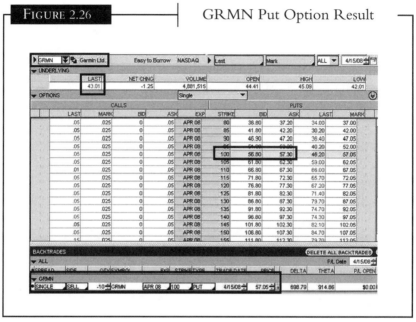

FIGURE 2.26   GRMN Put Option Result

For color charts go to: www.traderslibrary.com/TLECorner • Chart by: thinkorswim.com

Now you know why I like trading the downside of the market more than the upside of the market—it drops faster and can increase your rate of return faster than when the market goes up.

Self-test questions

1. When purchasing call options, you're looking for the stock to move which direction?

    A. Sideways
    B. Up
    C. Down

2. An option contract controls how many shares of the under-lying stock?

    A. 50
    B. 100
    C. 1,000

3. Options expire what day of each month?

    A. Monday
    B. Thursday
    C. Friday

4. When referring to an option price, the equity portion of the option is known as?

    A. Time Value
    B. Extrinsic Value
    C. Intrinsic Value

5. If you were to purchase a call option with a strike price of $90 and the stock was trading at $94, what would this option be considered?

    A. In-the-Money
    B. At-the-Money
    C. Out-of-the-Money

6. When purchasing a call option, you can lose more than the cost of the option.

    A. True
    B. False

7. The purchase of a call option gives you the buyer the right to do which of the following?

    A. Buy the stock
    B. Sell the stock
    C. Sell the option
    D. Both A and C

8. Of the three choices, which option costs more?

    A. In-the-Money
    B. At-the-Money
    C. Out-of-the-Money

9. An option price that is in-the-money will also have?

    A. Extrinsic Value
    B. Intrinsic Value
    C. A low Delta

10. When implied volatility increases, option prices do what?

    A. Decrease
    B. Increase
    C. Remain the same

For answers, go to www.traderslibrary.com/TLEcorner.

Three

It's All Greek To You: Understanding Delta, Gamma, and Theta

IN THIS CHAPTER

Importance of delta for calls and puts
How to use time decay (theta) to your advantage
Calculating the probability of expiring

IF YOU HAVE DONE research into option trading before, then chances are good that you've come across the Greeks. What are they and what do they have to do with option trading? Well, these terms refer to calculations made using an option pricing model (Black-Scholes for example) and tell an option trader how the price of an option will change (theoretically) given certain market variables. You don't really need to worry too much about the mathematics behind these calculations. The main thing is that you understand the concepts.

> **INSIDER SECRET**
>
> To calculate the theoretical values of the Greeks, you can use the option pricing models on www.thinkorswim.com for free.

Option Greeks will help you estimate your risk when trading options. Understanding the Greeks will enable you to answer certain questions about an option contract's expected price behavior, such as: how will the value of the option change as the stock price changes (delta); how fast will the option lose value as it approaches expiration (theta); what effect will a change in the stock's volatility have on the option value (vega); how will the delta of an option change relative to a one point move in the underlying asset (gamma)? There is fair amount of theory behind option pricing and a discussion of the formulas used is beyond the scope of this book, but I'll explain the basic definitions of the Greeks and, more important, help you understand how and why you should use them. Let's first begin with delta.

DELTA

Delta helps an option trader determine how much the option price will change based on every one dollar move of the underlying stock. If your selected option has delta of .60, then you know that for every one dollar your stock moves up, your option price will increase by a value of $.60 a share, or $60 for one contract. Note that calls and puts have opposite deltas. Call options are positive and put options are negative, which means that a call option will increase in value a certain amount as the stock moves up, and a put option will increase in value a certain amount as the underlying stock drops in value. Let's take a minute to review the Greeks chart so you'll have a visual understanding of delta.

Figure 3.1 will highlight what the recent current delta numbers are for each strike price for both the call and put options and the expiration months of February and March. Using this example for the stock Coca-Cola (KO), which has a current stock price of $60.74, you can see the various delta numbers that represent how much your selected option (strike price) will increase if you purchase a call or put option. For example, if you were to purchase the March $50 call option for the ask price of $11.60, you would look to the left and see a current delta of $.90. This number is telling us that for

FIGURE 3.1 — Delta Call Example

| | CALLS | | | KO Coca-Cola Co 60.74 0.00 0.00% | | PUTS | | | |
DELTA	MARK	BID X	ASK X	EXP	STRIKE	BID X	ASK X	DELTA	MARK
.98	15.85	15.60 X	16.10 X	FEB 08	45	0 B	.05 I	-.01	.025
.97	13.40	13.20 X	13.60 X	FEB 08	47.5	0 B	.05 I	-.01	.025
.95	10.95	10.80 I	11.10 I	FEB 08	50	0 B	.10 I	-.02	.05
.92	8.55	8.40 I	8.70 I	FEB 08	52.5	.10 I	.15 I	-.05	.125
.86	6.25	6.10 X	6.40 X	FEB 08	55	.25 I	.35 I	-.11	.30
.76	4.05	3.90 X	4.20 X	FEB 08	57.5	.60 I	.70 I	-.23	.65
.58	2.30	2.25 X	2.35 C	FEB 08	60	1.30 X	1.45 I	-.41	1.375
.17	.375	.35 C	.40 I	FEB 08	65	4.40 X	4.60 I	-.85	4.50
.03	.05	0 B	.10 I	FEB 08	70	9.10 C	9.40 X	-1.00	9.25
.96	16.05	15.80 I	16.30 X	MAY 08	45	.15 I	.20 I	-.04	.175
.93	13.75	13.60 I	13.90 X	MAY 08	47.5	.25 I	.35 I	-.06	.30
.90	11.45	11.30 I	11.60 X	MAY 08	50	.40 I	.50 I	-.09	.45
.85	9.25	9.10 X	9.40 I	MAY 08	52.5	.70 I	.80 I	-.14	.75
.78	7.20	7.10 X	7.30 I	MAY 08	55	1.15 B	1.20 N	-.21	1.175
.69	5.40	5.30 I	5.50 I	MAY 08	57.5	1.75 X	1.90 I	-.31	1.825
.58	3.80	3.70 X	3.90 I	MAY 08	60	2.65 X	2.80 I	-.42	2.725
.45	2.50	2.45 B	2.55 I	MAY 08	62.5	3.90 X	4.10 I	-.54	4.00
.33	1.525	1.45 X	1.60 X	MAY 08	65	5.40 X	5.70 I	-.67	5.55
.14	.475	.45 X	.50 I	MAY 08	70	9.40 X	9.70 I	-.86	9.55

For color charts go to: www.traderslibrary.com/TLECorner • Chart by: thinkorswim.com

every one dollar Coca-Cola's stock increases in value, the selected $50 call option will increase another $.90, which brings the current value of the March $50 call option to a new price of $12.50 ($11.60 + $.90).

I want you to notice that the further in-the-money your option is the greater the delta, and the further out-of-the-money the less the delta. When determining which call option to purchase, you'll need to give serious consideration to how far the stock will increase before it reaches its expiration date. Knowing that the $50 call option has a delta of $.90, you can anticipate how far you'll need the stock to increase to your ideal rate of return or profit. It's crucial that you use your charts and determine this before you purchase the option. If the stock is trading at $60.74 and it's reaching a current high, I'd wait for the stock to break up through the resistance because most stocks have a tendency to move lower after reaching these highs.

FIGURE 3.2 — Delta Put Example

| | CALLS | | | KO Coca-Cola Co 60.74 0.00 0.00% | | PUTS | | | |
DELTA	MARK	BID X	ASK X	EXP	STRIKE	BID X	ASK X	DELTA	MARK
.98	15.85	15.60 X	16.10 X	FEB 08	45	0 B	.05 I	-.01	.025
.97	13.40	13.20 X	13.60 X	FEB 08	47.5	0 B	.05 I	-.01	.025
.95	10.95	10.80 I	11.10 I	FEB 08	50	0 B	.10 I	-.02	.05
.92	8.55	8.40 I	8.70 I	FEB 08	52.5	.10 I	.15 I	-.05	.125
.86	6.25	6.10 X	6.40 X	FEB 08	55	.25 I	.35 I	-.11	.30
.76	4.05	3.90 X	4.20 X	FEB 08	57.5	.60 I	.70 I	-.23	.65
.58	2.30	2.25 X	2.35 C	FEB 08	60	1.30 X	1.45 I	-.41	1.375
.17	.375	.35 C	.40 I	FEB 08	65	4.40 X	4.60 I	-.85	4.50
.03	.05	0 B	.10 I	FEB 08	70	9.10 C	9.40 X	-1.00	9.25
.96	16.05	15.80 I	16.30 X	MAY 08	45	.15 I	.20 I	-.04	.175
.93	13.75	13.60 I	13.90 X	MAY 08	47.5	.25 I	.35 I	-.06	.30
.90	11.45	11.30 I	11.60 X	MAY 08	50	.40 I	.50 I	-.09	.45
.85	9.25	9.10 X	9.40 I	MAY 08	52.5	.70 I	.80 I	-.14	.75
.78	7.20	7.10 X	7.30 I	MAY 08	55	1.15 B	1.20 N	-.21	1.175
.69	5.40	5.30 I	5.50 I	MAY 08	57.5	1.75 X	1.90 I	-.31	1.825
.58	3.80	3.70 X	3.90 I	MAY 08	60	2.65 X	2.80 I	-.42	2.725
.45	2.50	2.45 B	2.55 I	MAY 08	62.5	4.40 I		-.54	4.00
.33	1.525	1.45 X	1.60 X	MAY 08	65	5.40 X	5.70 I	-.67	5.55
.14	.475	.45 X	.50 I	MAY 08	70	9.40 X	9.70 I	-.86	9.55

For color charts go to: www.traderslibrary.com/TLECorner • Chart by: thinkorswim.com

Now let's cover the deltas for put options, which are referred to as negative deltas because the delta number represents how much a put option investment will increase for every one dollar the stock drops. Taking the example of the May $65 put option (Figure 3.2), you'll see a delta of $.67. This number means that for every one dollar the stock price drops, our put option investment will increase by the amount of $.67. So, if we were to purchase this put option for the ask price of $5.70 and the stock dropped $3, our option would increase from $5.70 to $7.71 or [($.67 x $3) + $5.70 = $7.71)].

THETA

Theta shows how much value the option price will lose for every day that passes. An option contract has a finite life, defined by the expiration date. As the option approaches its maturity date, an option contract's expected value becomes more certain with each day. This time value, also called extrinsic value, represents the uncer-

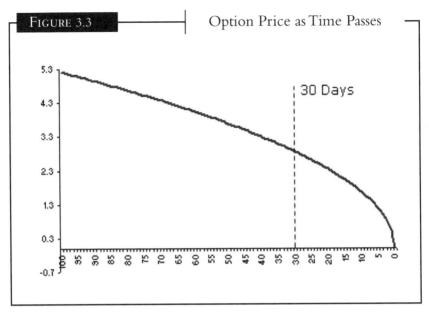

FIGURE 3.3 — Option Price as Time Passes

For color charts go to: www.traderslibrary.com/TLECorner • Chart by: thinkorswim.com

tainty of an option. Theta is the calculation that shows how much of this time value is eroding as each trading day passes—assuming all other inputs remain unchanged. Because of this negative impact on an option price, the theta will always be a negative number. For example, say an option has a theoretical price of $3.50 and is showing a theta value of -0.20. Tomorrow, if the underlying market opens unchanged (i.e., if it opens at the same price as the previous day's close), then the theoretical value of the option will now be worth $3.30 ($3.50 - $0.20).

The option graph in Figure 3.3 illustrates the effect on an OTM call option as it approaches maturity date. The increment as each day passes is what the theta calculates. You will notice that in the last remaining days of an option's life, it loses its value quite rapidly. This is one of the concepts traders use as a reason to short (sell) option contracts; they want to take advantage of this rapid rate of decay in an option's value as each trading day passes.

Looking at a February $85 call option for the stock Rimm (Figure 3.4), you'll see the theta for the call option is -12, which shows that the ask price of $8.55 will erode away at the rate of $.12 per day. Keep in mind that this theta number will also increase the closer that the option gets to its February expiration date. This is what we call time decay, meaning you're losing this theta amount every day and even more so if the stock doesn't move higher and you own the call option.

Perhaps you now can see why investors prefer to sell options instead of purchase—theta is melting away to their advantage, and this becomes a profit, not an expense. This is why writing a covered call or selling a put option is an alternative to buying options. We will cover great examples of selling time (theta) in later chapters on selling put options, bull put and bear call spreads, and iron condors.

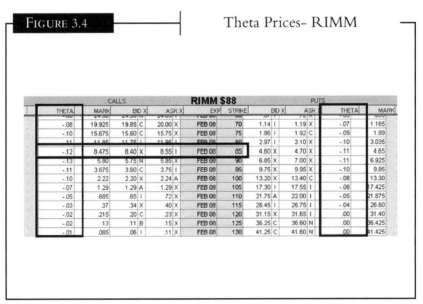

FIGURE 3.4   Theta Prices- RIMM

For color charts go to: www.traderslibrary.com/TLECorner • Chart by: thinkorswim.com

GAMMA

The gamma of an option indicates how the delta of an option will change relative to a one point move in the underlying asset. In other words, the gamma shows the option delta's sensitivity to market price changes. Gamma is important because it shows us how fast our delta will change as the market price of the underlying asset changes. Remember that one of the things the delta of an option tells us is effectively how many underlying contracts we are long/short. So, the gamma is telling us how fast our "effective" underlying position will change. In other words, gamma shows how volatile an option is relative to movements in the underlying asset. By watching your gamma, you will know how much your delta (position risk) changes.

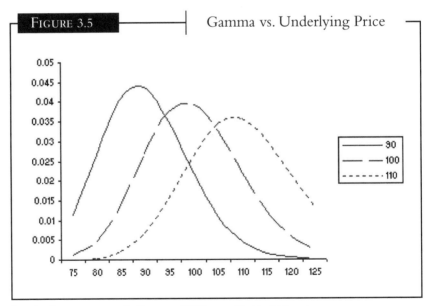

For color charts go to: www.traderslibrary.com/TLECorner • Chart by: thinkorswim.com

The gamma graph shows Gamma vs. Underlying Price for three different strike prices (Figure 3.5). You can see that gamma increases as the option moves from in-the-money and then reaches its peak at-the-money. As the option moves out-of-the-money, the gamma then decreases.

Please note that the gamma value is the same for calls as for puts. If you are long a call or a put, the gamma will be a positive number. If you are short a call or a put, the gamma will be a negative number. When you are "long gamma," your position will become "longer" as the price of the underlying asset increases and "shorter" as the underlying price decreases.

Conversely, if you sell options, and are therefore "short gamma," your position will become shorter as the underlying price increases and longer as the underlying decreases. This is an important distinction to make between being long or short options—both calls and puts. That is, when you are long an option (long gamma), you want the market to move. As the underlying price increases, you become longer, which reinforces your newly long position. If being long gamma means you want movements in the underlying asset, then being short gamma means that you do not want the price of the underlying asset to move. A short gamma position will become shorter as the price of the underlying asset increases. As the market rallies, you are effectively selling more and more of the underlying asset as the delta becomes more negative.

PROBABILITY OF EXPIRING

We could spend hours talking about the various Greeks and how they will affect your option investments; however, I have found a tool that really summarizes them all. It's the "Probability of Expiring." This is by far my favorite tool when it comes to calculating the

FIGURE 3.6 ─────┤   Probability of Expiring ─────

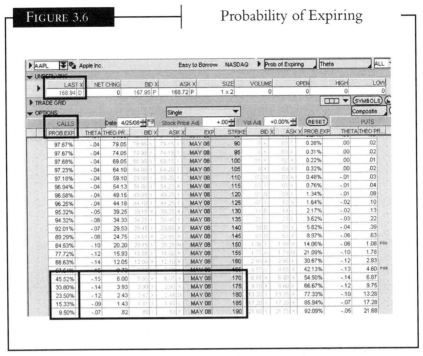

For color charts go to: www.traderslibrary.com/TLECorner • Chart by: thinkorswim.com

effect the Greeks will have on any option, and what the percentage is for any particular option to expire.

Using Figure 3.6, we'll look at the call options for the strike prices ranging from 170 to 190. As you'll notice, with each of the different strike prices there is a percentage number under the PROB EXP tab, which indicates what the percentage of the option is expiring in-the-money.

The 170 call option has a probability of expiring percentage of 45.52, which means that there is a 54.48% chance that the stock will remain below the 170 price and a 9.50% chance that the stock will go above the 190 price come expiration. Looking at Figure 3.7, we'll view the probability of expiring for the put options.

FIGURE 3.7 Probability of Expiring for a Put Option

AAPL — Apple Inc. — Easy to Borrow — NASDAQ — Prob of Expiring — Theta — ALL

UNDERLYING

LAST X	NET CHNG	BID X	ASK X	SIZE	VOLUME	OPEN	HIGH	LOW
168.94 D	0	167.95 P	168.72 P	1 x 2	0	0	0	0

TRADE GRID

OPTIONS — Single — Composite — SYMBOLS

Date 4/25/08 — Stock Price Adj +.00 — Vol Adj +0.00% — RESET

CALLS PROB.EXP	THETA	THEO PR..	BID X	ASK X	EXP	STRIKE	PUTS BID X	ASK X	PROB.EXP	THETA	THEO PR..
97.67%	-.04	79.05	78.95 I	79.15 I	MAY 08	90	0 X	.03 C	0.28%	.00	.02
97.67%	-.04	74.05	73.95 I	74.15 I	MAY 08	95	0 X	.03 I	0.31%	.00	.02
97.68%	-.04	69.05	68.95 I	69.15 I	MAY 08	100	.01 X	.02 X	0.22%	.00	.01
97.23%	-.04	64.10	64.00 I	64.20 I	MAY 08	105	0 X	.03 X	0.32%	.00	.02
97.18%	-.04	59.10	59.00 I	59.20 I	MAY 08	110	.02 N	.03 A	0.48%	-.01	.03
96.94%	-.04	54.13	54.00 I	54.25 X	MAY 08	115	.03 I	.05 I	0.76%	-.01	.04
96.58%	-.04	49.15	49.05 I	49.25 I	MAY 08	120	.07 N	.09 I	1.34%	-.01	.08
96.25%	-.04	44.18	44.10 I	44.25 I	MAY 08	125	.07 I	.12 X	1.64%	-.02	.10
95.32%	-.05	39.25	39.15 X	39.35 X	MAY 08	130	.11 B	.14 C	2.17%	-.02	.13
94.32%	-.06	34.33	34.25 I	34.40 I	MAY 08	135	.21 C	.23 I	3.62%	-.03	.22
92.01%	-.07	29.53	29.45 I	29.60 X	MAY 08	140	.38 B	.39 I	5.82%	-.04	.39
89.29%	-.08	24.75	24.65 X	24.85 X	MAY 08	145	.61 N	.65 X	8.97%	-.06	.63
84.53%	-.10	20.20	20.15 I	20.25 N	MAY 08	150	1.06 I	1.10 X	14.06%	-.08	1.08
77.72%	-.12	15.93	15.85 I	16.00 X	MAY 08	155	1.77 A	1.79 N	21.09%	-.10	1.78
68.63%	-.14	12.05	12.00 X	12.10 X	MAY 08	160	2.90 A	2.95 I	30.67%	-.12	2.93
57.54%	-.15	8.73	8.65 X	8.80 I	[illegible]	[illegible]	[illegible]	[illegible]	[illegible]	[illegible]	[illegible]
45.52%	-.15	6.00	5.95 X	6.05 X	MAY 08	170	6.85 X	6.90 X	54.50%	-.14	6.87
33.80%	-.14	3.93	3.90 I	3.95 X	MAY 08	175	9.70 X	9.80 I	66.67%	-.12	9.75
23.50%	-.12	2.43	2.42 X	2.44 N	MAY 08	180	13.20 I	13.35 X	77.33%	-.10	13.28
15.33%	-.09	1.43	1.41 I	1.45 C	MAY 08	185	17.20 I	17.35 X	85.94%	-.07	17.28
9.50%	-.07	.82	.80 I	.83 X	MAY 08	190	21.60 I	21.75 X	92.09%	-.05	21.68

For color charts go to: www.traderslibrary.com/TLECorner • Chart by: thinkorswim.com

The 170 put option shows a percentage of 54.50, which tells us that the stock has a 55.50% chance of expiring in-the-money. For put option, this means the stock would need to be above the 170 strike price in order to be in-the-money. Now, if you'll look at the 190 strike price, you'll see 92.09%, which again tells us that the stock has a 92.09% chance of expiring in the money (below $190). With the stock trading at about $169, the probability calculator tells us the stock should remain below the 190 price come expiration date.

The use of a probability calculator is fairly new to many traders yet if properly used, it can become an extremely important tool for option traders. To better explain the use of this powerful tool keep in mind that the probability percentage given for a call option tells us the percentage of the stock staying below our chosen price come expiration day. As for the put option side it tells us what the percentage is of the stock closing below our chosen price. To give you an easy concept let's say that you were looking to buy a call option on XYZ stock, and it was trading at $46 per share. If you chose an option strike price of $40 and the probability of expiring number was 38%, then you had a 62% chance that the stock price of $46 would remain above your strike price of $40 come expiration. As the stock price increases, the probability of expiring decreases, which increases your odds of that stock staying above the $40 price.

It's the same concept for a put option except we're looking at the odds of the stock closing *below* the chosen strike price come expiration day. Assume you're bearish on a stock. While the stock was trading at $98 per share, you purchased the $100 put option, which had a probability number of 57%. This means you only have a 53% chance that the stock ($98) will remain below the $100 strike price come expiration day. As the stock price drops in value, your probability of being successful will increase because your goal when purchasing a put option is for the stock to drop in value and as it does, your investment increases. As an option trader it is always helpful to refer to the probability of expiring percentage once you've determined your investment strategy.

Self-test questions

1. When trading options, the Greeks can be very helpful. The Greek "delta" tells us what?

    A. When the option will expire

    B. How much the option is over-priced

    C. How much the option will move when the stock moves

2. Theta tells us what about an option?

    A. How much the delta will increase for every one dollar the stock increases

    B. How fast the option premium will melt away

    C. How much equity is within our option

3. Sellers of an option prefer to see theta that is what?

    A. High

    B. Low

4. If you were looking for the price of a stock to increase $5, which delta would have the greatest increase on your option price?

    A. Delta of .50

    B. Delta of .60

    C. Delta of .90

5. If your option's probability of expiring is 32%, we know that the option has a 32% chance of expiring what?

    A. In-the-Money

    B. At-the-Money

    C. Out-of-the-Money

6. When looking at the probability of expiring percentage, if the percentage number is low, then you'd rather be?

    A. The buyer of the option
    B. The seller of the option
    C. Neither the buyer or the seller

7. Gamma has a price effect on which of the following Greeks?

    A. Beta
    B. Theta
    C. Delta

8. As a call option approaches its expiration date, the option that will have the greatest decrease in theta value will be the option that is what?

    A. In-the-Money
    B. At-the-Money
    C. Out-of-the-Money

9. The use of the various option Greeks can best help an investor determine?

    A. The direction of the option
    B. The risk of an option
    C. The potential profit or loss on an option

10. When using the term "short gamma," you need the underlying investment to go in which direction for your investment to increase in value?

    A. Up
    B. Sideways
    C. Down

For answers, go to www.traderslibrary.com/TLEcorner.

Four

Making the Call: Buying Call Options

IN THIS CHAPTER

Identifying bullish trends
Purchasing time
Making a few trades for big returns

Let's review: the purchase of a call option is the right (not the obligation) to purchase the underlying stock for a certain price known as the strike price, on or before a certain date (expiration date). Knowing this, we'll be looking for bullish stocks in uptrending markets, selecting the best available call option for purchase, and selling the option for a profit if we were right. If not, we need to be willing to sell the option at a loss if the stock goes down instead of up. In many ways this strategy is the same as real estate investment during good times, such 2000 though 2005.

As an example, if we were to purchase a June $70 call option for $5 and the stock moved to $80, the $70 strike price would have a minimum value of $10; so, instead of buying the stock for $70 per share when it is worth $80 per share, we would sell the option for $10 to close out the trade. We would make $5 per share or 100% return on our option investment of $5.

THINK REAL ESTATE

Buying call options is similar to a real estate lease option; you're willing to sell your home, and I'm willing to purchase it. So, I purchase a contract giving me the right to purchase your home for a certain price on or before a certain date. I pay you a premium for this option to purchase. Several important parts of this contract are the time frame (expiration date) and the price I agree to pay for the home (strike price). Let's say I was to give you $3,000 with 60 days to buy your house for $400,000. I now have three choices and must do one of the three before the expiration date.

1. I exercise my right and pay you $400,000 before the expiration date and I own the house (or the stock).

2. I don't exercise my right and allow you to keep the house and my option investment of $3,000. My maximum loss is $3,000.

3. I sell my option to someone else, allowing them to exercise the right to purchase the house (stock) before the expiration date for the price of $400,000. In many cases if the value of the house (stock) increased, our option did as well; so, when we sell the option, our profit is the net difference between the $3,000 we paid for the option and the selling price of the option.

Before I talk about how it really works within the stock market, let's review why each of the three choices are different. When referring to example number one (where you exercised your option), you have now agreed to purchase the house for $400,000. At the time of the option agreement, you were looking for the value of the home to increase above the $400,000 value. So, let's say that the home is now worth $450,000. You invested $3,000 for the option and you purchased the home for $400,000; therefore, you now have an increased profit of $47,000.

Purchase price (strike): $400,000
Premium for the option to purchase: $3,000
New value of home (stock price): $450,000
Profit: [450,000-400,000] - 3,000 = $47,000

In our second example, we chose not to exercise our option and let the contract expire, losing only the option investment of $3,000. The reason: the value of the home dropped from $400,000 to a value of $350,000; so, losing the premium of $3,000 is much better than buying the house at $50,000 less in value.

Purchase price (strike): $400,000
Premium for the option to purchase: $3,000
New value of home (stock price): $350,000
Profit: 0
Loss at expiration (premium): $3,000

The reason I would invest short-term in real estate or with stocks is so I can watch the value of the investment increase, which will allow me to sell the option to someone else, take my profit, and move on to another investment.

This is leverage at its best: you controlled the house (stock) until you were ready to sell the option and because the house (stock) increased in value, the option price did as well. With the click of a button, you sold the option for the bid price, which in our example was a profit of $47 per share. It's important to remember that your investment must increase in value in order for your option price to increase in value. If the investment doesn't increase enough, then you could still lose your option premium as well come expiration day.

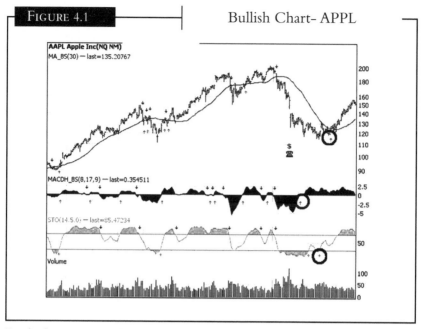

FIGURE 4.1 — Bullish Chart- APPL

For color charts go to: www.traderslibrary.com/TLECorner • Chart by: thinkorswim.com

THE POWER OF BUYING CALLS

BULLISH ON APPLE

Let's begin examining the power of buying a call option (Figure 4.1). As you'll see within the chart, we identified a bullish upward movement with the use of three circled arrows on the technical indicator chart (Moving Average, MACD, Stochastics).

As you'll notice, the buy signal occurred at about the $120 price when the stock moved above the moving average, while the other two indicators also showed bullish signals (circled). Now, after identifying that the stock can move higher, we can use the Greeks to determine which option to purchase and what time frame and strike price would be best.

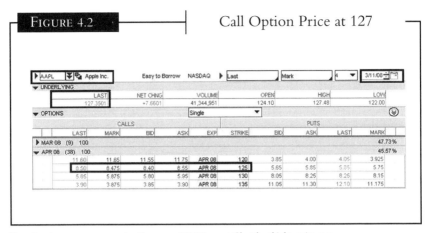

For color charts go to: www.traderslibrary.com/TLECorner • Chart by: thinkorswim.com

Figure 4.2 shows the value of the $125 call option for April at an ask price of $8.55 per share ($855 per contract). Compare that cost to the purchase price of 100 shares outright for a total cost of $12,700. Which would you rather do: make an investment of $855 or $12,700? I hope you said $855 because that is truly the value of using leverage within the stock market.

Let's compare Figures 4.2 and 4.3. You'll see that the stock increased from $127 to $155, and the April 125 call option increased from $8.55 to $31.05 in less than 30 days, giving us a profit of $22.50 per share ($2,250 for one contract) with a 263% return! This is compared to a $2,800 profit and 22% return if you had bought the stock itself.

More important, we didn't tie up a large amount of our funds to purchase the stock, which allows us to use the remaining funds toward other investments. Of equal importance, we placed a trade on a very expensive stock, yet we had limited risk of only $855 for one contract (100 shares). This is a perfect example of the third scenario we discussed earlier. We had the ability to purchase a call option to

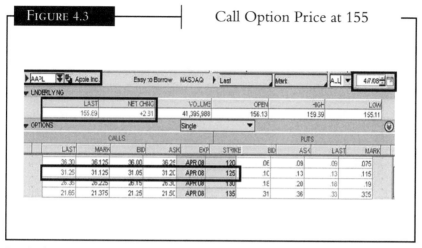

For color charts go to: www.traderslibrary.com/TLECorner • Chart by: thinkorswim.com

buy the stock at a certain price (strike price) on or before a certain date (expiration date); yet, our desire wasn't to buy the stock but to benefit on the upward movement. When the stock moved up, we elected to sell the option at the current bid price and give someone else the opportunity to exercise the right and purchase the stock. We get to take the profit and move on to the next opportunity.

Keep in mind that these are not the type of trades you'll be doing all the time; I refer to this style as the "get rich" bag because when you're wrong, and you will be at times, you can lose the entire cost of the option. A few of these every month will be really rewarding and, with good money man-agement, you'll continue to take the proceeds and move them into more conservative trades like debit or credit spreads, which tend to be a bit more forgiving.

> **INSIDER SECRET**
>
> Making a few aggres-sive trades a month with your "get rich" bag of money becomes rewarding when you can make that extra income continue to work for you in more conservative trades.

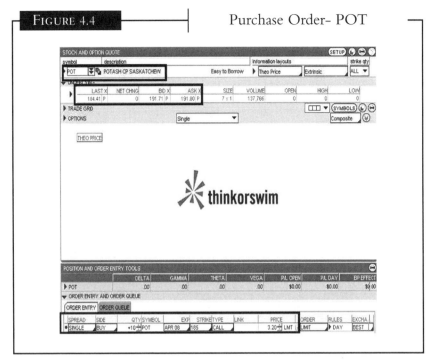

FIGURE 4.4 — Purchase Order- POT

For color charts go to: www.traderslibrary.com/TLECorner • Chart by: thinkorswim.com

BULLISH ON POTASH

Our next example (Figure 4.4) involves a stock that has really been on fire and has moved up quickly within a 12-month period beginning at $50 per share and reaching close to $200 per share. The 185 April call option cost $3.20 per share ($320 per contract) and within a few weeks, the stock moved from $184 to $197. That means the April 185 call option increased to a value of $13 per share (or $1,300 per contract).

Cost to Buy Option: $3,200 per 10 contracts
Sell Price at End of Trade: $13,000 per 10 contracts
Profit: 13,000- 3,200 = 9,800
Rate of Return: (9,800 / 3,200) x 100 = 306%

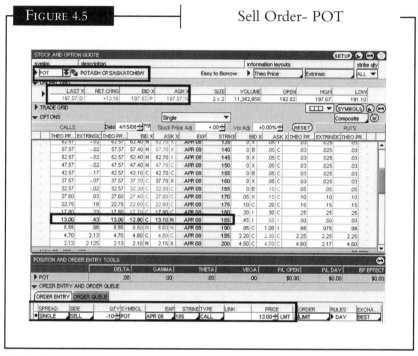

FIGURE 4.5 | Sell Order- POT

For color charts go to: www.traderslibrary.com/TLECorner • Chart by: thinkorswim.com

Figure 4.5 shows the selling order for the call option. Based on 10 contracts, you had a cost of $3,200 and a selling price of $13,000. Your rate of return would then be 306%, or $9,800 in profit.

These are the type of trades for which I'm willing to risk a portion of my "get rich" account because when you're right, the reward is increasingly better then any other strategy.

PURCHASING MORE TIME

This next example of Potash (Figure 4.6) uses the same strike price of 185 but instead of a short-term April option, we purchased the May 185 call option for a price of $13.30 per share equaling $1,330 per contract. This allows more time for the stock and option to in-

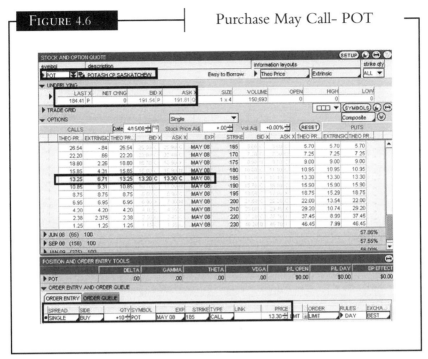

FIGURE 4.6 — Purchase May Call- POT

For color charts go to: www.traderslibrary.com/TLECorner • Chart by: thinkorswim.com

crease in price before the third Friday of May, which is the expiration date of the option.

If you'll look at Figure 4.7, you'll see the current price of the $185 May call option is $20.80 per share. When the stock moved from $184.41 to $197.57, it increased the call option value from a purchase price of $13.30 to the current price of $20.80. If you were to sell this May call option right now, your profit would be $7.50 per share or $750 per contract, equaling a 56% rate of return. This is another great trade for your high risk, "get rich" money bag.

But wait! At the time of writing, I was a strong believer that the stock would move higher in the next few weeks, allowing me to increase my profit on the call option.

FIGURE 4.7 — Current Price Four Weeks Before Expiration (POT)

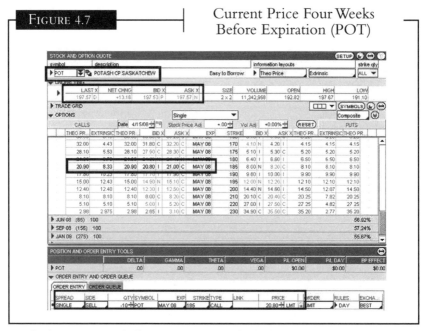

For color charts go to: www.traderslibrary.com/TLECorner • Chart by: thinkorswim.com

FIGURE 4.8 — Final Call Option For POT

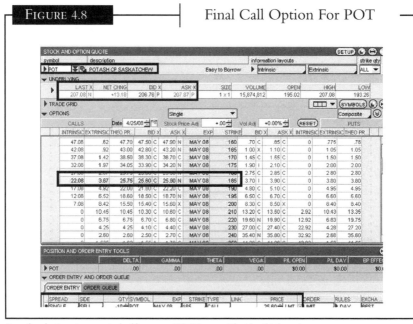

For color charts go to: www.traderslibrary.com/TLECorner • Chart by: thinkorswim.com

As you can see in Figure 4.8, the 185 May Call option increased and is now trading at $25.60 per share ($2,560 per contract), which grew our profits from $20.80 per share to $25.60. This is an additional gain of $4.80 per share, or $480 per contract. From our initial price of $13.30, we have now increased our rate of return from 56% to 92%, and the option still has another 2 weeks before its expiration date. In our next section, I'll be using two of my favorite technical indicators (10- and 20-day moving averages and Inertia), which I covered in chapter one. You'll get a quick look as I reference the most recent buy (bullish) signals.

THE KEYS TO SUCCESSFUL CALL OPTION TRADES

The last portion of this chapter deals with my ideas as to why stocks move up at such rapid speeds, such as Potash did. If you're looking to increase your odds of making money with the purchase of call options, then you may want to set up your own checklist of rules to follow and develop your money management skills. Each of the following examples represents what I believe is the true story of being a successful call option trader. View each of them and come to your own conclusions. But, I hope that your conclusions are close to mine and that this section gives you the confidence to be a successful option trader.

CHECK THE CHARTS

Beginning with Figure 4.9, a basic chart shows us that the stock has been in a bullish upward trend for the past 12 months. We'll need to determine when to buy the call options and when not to. Let's start with a simple rule: a recent arrow on the moving average, MACD, and Stochastics (review chapter one for more information) along with a break of resistance. It's important that you wait for stocks to break up through their resistance; it will increase your odds of the

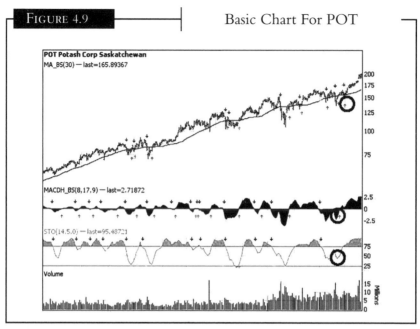

FIGURE 4.9 — Basic Chart For POT

For color charts go to: www.traderslibrary.com/TLECorner • Chart by: thinkorswim.com

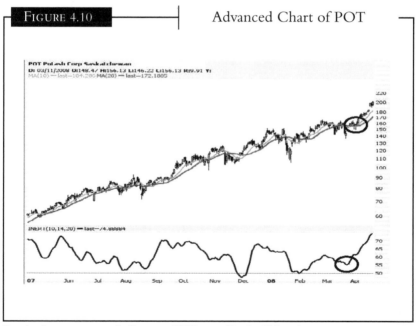

FIGURE 4.10 — Advanced Chart of POT

For color charts go to: www.traderslibrary.com/TLECorner • Chart by: thinkorswim.com

stock moving higher because this often is a sign that institutional investors are buying more stock. This will continue to increase the price.

On our next chart (Figure 4.10), I'm using two of my favorite technical indicators (10- and 20-day moving averages and inertia), which I covered in chapter one. Here, you get a quick look as I reference the most recent buy (bullish) signals.

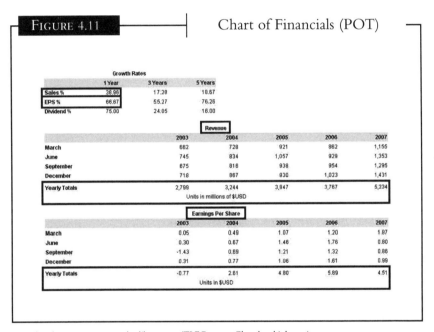

FIGURE 4.11 — Chart of Financials (POT)

CHECK THE FINANCIALS

In our next example (Figure 4.11), you get a quick look at the company's financials, which are an important part of a stock's bullish success, especially when a stock has moved up so far so fast. The five things that I look for within a strong financial company are their: 1) sales percentage increase (over the past one year); 2) Earnings Per

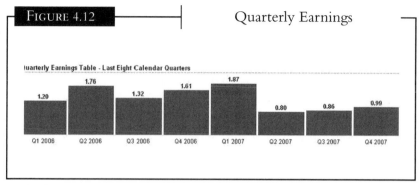

Share (EPS) increase of the past one year; 3) EPS greater than sales percentage (based on the past one year); 4) increasing revenue year over year for the past five years; and 5) EPS increasing year over year for the past five years.

CHECK THE EARNINGS

We also need to look at the actual chart and numbers of the company's earnings for the past two years (eight quarters). In Figure 4.12, we can see not only how well the company has done, but we can also get a visual of their strongest and weakest quarters of the year. More important, I'm looking for weakness in their recent quarter. If the most recent quarter shows signs of weakness, then I'll need to be careful and set tighter exits for my call option in case the stock begins a downward fall.

CHECK THE INDUSTRY GROUP

The most important aspect of any stock movement will be the industry group. With the use of two different charts, we're able to track the strength of the industry group as well as the three-month ranking for the individual industry. Figure 4.13 shows that the Non-Metallic Mining Industry has been moving up in the past 12 months, and the group as a whole has increased from 2,500 to

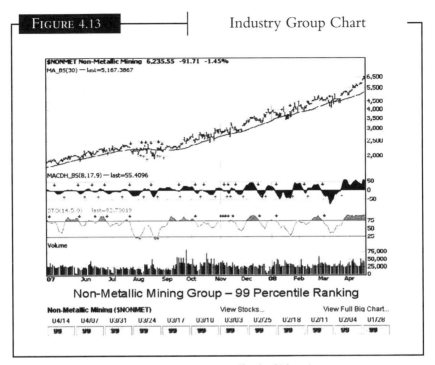

For color charts go to: www.traderslibrary.com/TLECorner • Chart by: thinkorswim.com

6,500, representing the total price of all the stocks that are in the same industry group.

This chart simply tells us that institutional money has moved into these stocks over the past year, which is a primary reason that a stock such as Potash has done so well. Keep in mind that when institutional money moves into a certain selected industry group, stocks within that group will have a 50% increase in their stock price and visa versa. When institutional money comes out of an industry group, stocks within the group can drop 50% in value.

The bottom section shows that the Non-Metallic Mining Group is currently in the 99-percentile ranking each week from January 28 through the week of April 14. This tells us that Non-Metallic Mining is one of the groups that institutional money is in or continuing to move into, which means that we can expect many of the stocks within this group to show great signs of upward strength. That is until the institutional money comes out of this group, at which time many of the stocks within the Non-Metallic Mining Group will drop at least 50% in value.

Knowing that Potash is one of the stocks within this group and trading at about $200 per share, it will drop in value at least $100 per share when the large investors take their profits and sell the stocks within this group. A key rule to remember is that you

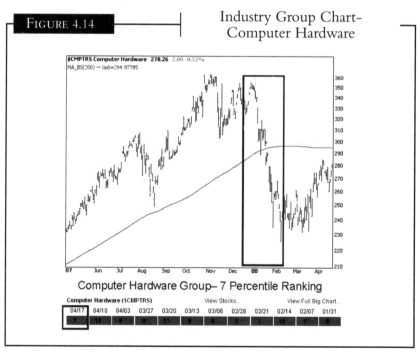

FIGURE 4.14 — Industry Group Chart–Computer Hardware

For color charts go to: www.traderslibrary.com/TLECorner • Chart by: thinkorswim.com

116

and I do not move the markets up or down; but, because of today's technology, you and I have increased odds of being much more successful than in the past. Tools like this give us the ability to see what the largest investors are buying and selling, and where it only takes minutes to buy the quality of stock or options, it can take the largest investors several weeks or months to complete their entire trade whether they're buying or selling.

WATCH INSTITUTIONAL MONEY

To finish off this powerful chapter, I'm going to show you a few more examples of how institutional money can move even a good stock up or down quickly. Figure 4.14 shows both the industry group chart for the Computer Hardware Group and the Big Chart

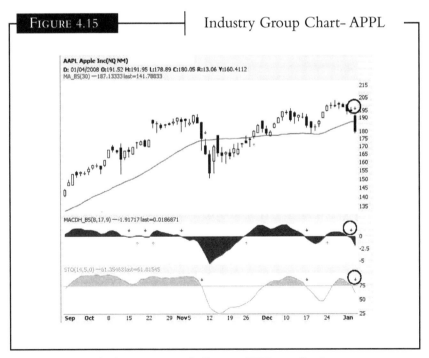

| FIGURE 4.15 | Industry Group Chart- APPL |

thinkorswim.com For color charts go to: www.traderslibrary.com/TLECorner • Chart by:

showing how institutional money moved out of the industry group at the end of December through April, proving that even a financially strong stock like Apple Computer can move down when the institutions want it to.

In the next example (Figure 4.15), Apple Computer moved down from a high of $200 to about $118 week over week as stocks within this group were sold. More important, you'll notice that the technical indicators within the chart showed three arrows at about $190 per share. This was telling you to sell your stock or be sure to have a stop loss (pre-determined order to sell at a certain price to avoid greater losses) in place to avoid greater losses if the stock continues to move lower.

CAUTION

When Buying Calls, Use Your "Get Rich" Bag

Please remember that the purchase of a call option is the right to buy the stock at a certain price on or before a certain date. My desire is not to buy the stock; I simply want to sell the option for a profit and move on to another trade. This is a higher risk trade and only a certain percentage of your investment net worth should be used for these types of trades.

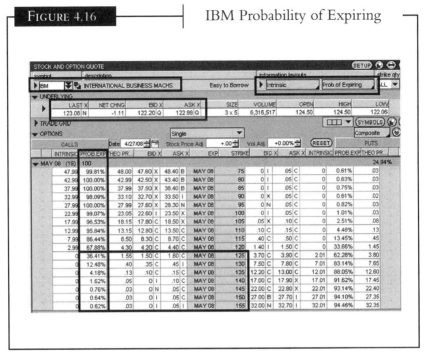

FIGURE 4.16 | IBM Probability of Expiring

For color charts go to: www.traderslibrary.com/TLECorner • Chart by: thinkorswim.com

PROBABILITY OF EXPIRING– BUYING CALL OPTIONS

Over the past several months, I have seen huge benefits to using the probability of expiring to evaluate an option before placing the trade. As a review, probability of expiring means the "chance of expiring in-the-money."

Let's begin this discussion with a visual. In Figure 4.16 you'll see that we have selected IBM and we are going to determine the probability of the out-of-the-money options expiring worthless. The number quoted tells us the chance of that particular option reaching that strike price; so, looking at the 125 through 155 strike prices, you'll see that the percentages range from 36.41% for the 125 call

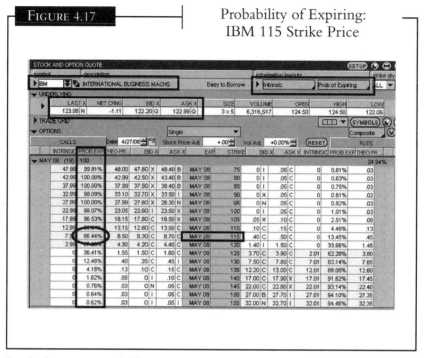

FIGURE 4.17   Probability of Expiring: IBM 115 Strike Price

For color charts go to: www.traderslibrary.com/TLECorner • Chart by: thinkorswim.com

option and 0.62% for the 155 strike price. Using the 125 strike price as an example, we know now that if we were to buy the call option for the May 125 strike price and paid the ask price of $1.60 per share, our option would have about a 36% chance of getting to $125 per share.

In our second example of IBM (Figure 4.17), you'll see that the 115 May strike price shows that the probability of expiring is 86.44%, meaning that it has about a 14% chance of closing below the 115 price on expiration day. Knowing your odds of success before making a trade will only increase your odds of actually becoming successful.

For the first time in my trading career such a powerful tool is now available, and I assure you, I will always look at an option's probabil-

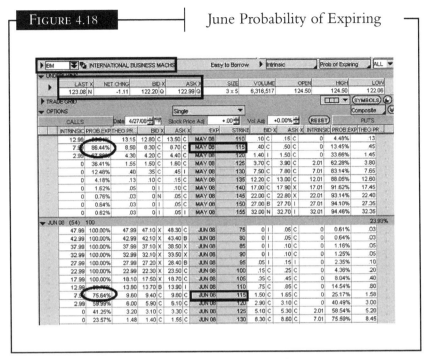

FIGURE 4.18 — June Probability of Expiring

For color charts go to: www.traderslibrary.com/TLECorner • Chart by: thinkorswim.com

ity of expiring before I place any trade. More important, I'll select a strike price and expiration month that will increase my odds of being profitable. For a better example of this, we'll now use the same information for IBM except we'll look at the June 115 strike price, which will allow more time before the option expires.

As you'll see in Figure 4.18, the June 115 call option has a 75% probability of expiring at or below the 115 price come expiration, which is lower than the May's 86% because the May option has only 2 weeks before expiring while the June option has 6 weeks. If the June 115 call option has a 75% probability of expiring, then we know that it has a 75% chance of being in-the-money and a 25% chance of closing below the $115 price.

As you read on, I want you to keep in mind what I've said several times, "it's best to be a seller and not a buyer." With that said, you'll see how the use of probability of expiring will help us when we sell covered calls, sell naked puts, or place spread trades. If we know what the probability of an option expiring is, then we'll take advantage of that and be a seller of time premium instead of a buyer of time premium, such as we did here when buying call options.

HUGE RATES OF RETURN ARE POSSIBLE

Can call options give you the ability to benefit with huge rates of returns? Take a look at my final call option example, which is a one-day trade on Google. Figure 4.19 shows the purchase price

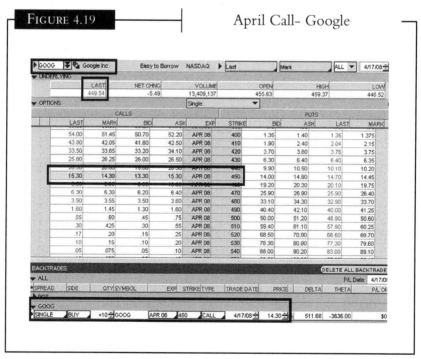

FIGURE 4.19   April Call- Google

For color charts go to: www.traderslibrary.com/TLECorner • Chart by: thinkorswim.com

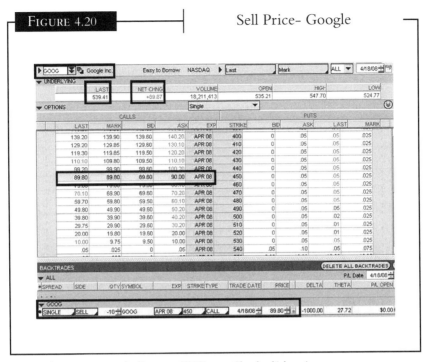

FIGURE 4.20   Sell Price- Google

For color charts go to: www.traderslibrary.com/TLECorner • Chart by: thinkorswim.com

of a $450 April call option the day before the April expiration and the day that Google was to release their earnings. The cost was $14.30, or $1,430 for one contract, when the stock was at $449.54. Now keep in mind, this option expires the following day, so this is a high risk one day trade. Use your "get rich" account because if the stock doesn't move up at least $14.30, you could lose the entire investment.

You can see the results of this trade in Figure 4.20 after the market closed Thursday. Google released positive earnings—the stock moved up $89.87 per share and the April $450 call option increased from $14.30 to $89.80. Based on one contract, your $1,430 investment generated a profit of $7,550, equaling a rate of return of 528% for one day. Now will this happen every day or every month? No, but a few of these every year would be a really nice way to build your "stay rich" account.

BUYING CALLS IS FOR BULLS

When I started trading in 1998, I focused on buying call options for two reasons; first, it took a lot less cash than buying the stocks during the 1998 and 1999 bull market, and second, I could calculate what my risk was before I placed the trade. Even though call options have less up front risk than buying stock, you must remember that the stock must move up for you to profit. You will be wrong at times, so I want to encourage you to only use call options during a bull market and on stocks that have great upside opportunity and never risk more than you can afford to lose.

This has to be one of, if not the best, chapter I've ever written. The information I've shared with you will greatly increase your chance at successfully trading call options.

Self-test questions

1. The purchase of call options should only be done on stocks that have?

    A. Upside potential
    B. Sideways potential
    C. Downward potential

2. When purchasing a call option, which one of the three is not true?

    A. Buy the stock at your selected call option price.
    B. Sell the call option at the current price.
    C. Sell your stock.

3. The selection of an in-the-money call option will cost _____ then an out-of-the-money option?

    A. More
    B. Less

4. When selecting a call option, you can choose a time frame as recent as the current month or as far out as what?

    A. Six months
    B. Twelve months
    C. Twenty-four months

5. True or false: The buyer of a call option must wait until the expiration date to exercise the right to purchase the stock or sell the option.

    A. True

    B. False

6. When buying a call option, which one of the following is the most important?

    A. Company financials

    B. Industry group

    C. Technical indicators

7. A call option can have both intrinsic and extrinsic value; which of the two is more important?

    A. Intrinsic Value

    B. Extrinsic Value

8. When determining which call option strike price you'd like to purchase, you should check the _____ to help determine the correct strike price.

    A. Gamma

    B. Theta

    C. Delta

9. When a stock has reached a resistance level (ceiling), it is best to purchase a call option before the stock breaks through the ceiling because the option will have less implied volatility and the cost of the call option will be less.

    A. True
    B. False

10. If a call option has a 75% probability of expiring, then we know it will:

    A. Have a 25% chance of making money.
    B. Have a 75% chance of losing money.
    C. Have a 75% chance of expiring in-the-money.

For answers, go to www.traderslibrary.com/TLEcorner.

Five

You Have It Covered: Covered Calls

IN THIS CHAPTER

Aspects of covered calls
Guidelines for writing
Examining the charts and the rate of return

The term covered call means you own the underlying stock and are going to sell an option against that underlying stock, which gives someone the right to purchase your stock from you for a certain price on or before your selected expiration date. Again, we will be trading contracts, which are groups of 100 shares.

Let's look at a short explanation and then go through several visual examples. Assume you own 1,000 shares of the stock XYZ, and the stock is trading at a current price of $23.50. About three weeks before the third Friday, you review the various strike prices for the current month (March) expiration, and see that a strike price of $25.00 is available. You sell 10 contracts of the March $25 option and receive the bid price of $.75 per share, which brings $750.00 into your account [$.75 x 1,000 shares].

COVERED CALL "WHAT IF" SCENARIOS

1. STOCK PRICE MOVES ABOVE YOUR CHOSEN STRIKE PRICE.

If the price of the stock moves above your chosen strike price of $25 at expiration, then your stock will be taken out of your account and sold to someone else at the price of $25 regardless of how much higher the stock price is. Taking this example, you have sold your stock for $25 per share plus you collected the option premium of $.75 per share for another $750.00.

2. STOCK PRICE REMAINS BELOW YOUR CHOSEN STRIKE PRICE.

Second, what if the stock remains below the $25 strike price at expiration day? You keep the stock and keep the option premium of $.75 per share times 1,000 shares or $750. So again, if the stock remains below the strike price of $25, you keep your 1,000 shares of stock and the option premium, which now generates additional income of $.75 per share for a stock that you already own.

3. STOCK PRICE DROPS IN VALUE AND SHOWS GREAT DOWNSIDE RISK.

Third, the stock drops in value and you still own the stock and keep the premium; but, what if the stock shows great downside risk and you'd like to sell the stock before the expiration date? You'll need to close out the option trade by buying back (buy to close) the exact option strike price for the exact expiration month. If this is something you see yourself doing, you must know that the cost to purchase the call option could be more or less than the premium you received. Often, when the stock drops, the cost is less. Regardless of the option cost, if you need to sell the stock, you'll have to close out the option trade because you can't sell the stock twice. For instance, say you write a covered call to sell the stock at $25 and then the stock drops to $23. You sell the stock at $23; yet, you still have the option, which gives someone the ability to buy the stock from you on or before the expiration date. The stock moves back above $25 but you don't own the stock because you sold it before the expiration date.

Covered Call Chart Examples

In our first covered call example (Figure 5.1), we'll use Visa (V) and sell an at-the-money call option for a premium of $4.15 (this premium is the mid-price, which is between the bid price of $4.00 and the ask price of $4.30) with an expiration of 3 weeks. Our goal will be for the stock to move above $75 per share. Then, we will sell the stock at $75 per share and keep the option premium of $4.15. Our

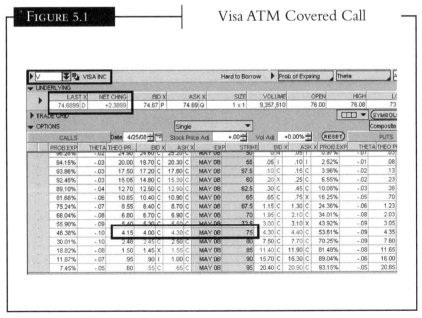

FIGURE 5.1 — Visa ATM Covered Call

For color charts go to: www.traderslibrary.com/TLECorner • Chart by: thinkorswim.com

rate of return on this trade is based on the cost of the stock ($74.69) and the selling price of $75 per share plus the option premium of $4.15, which equals a total profit of $4.46 and a rate of return of 5.9% for 3 weeks.

Think about this, your rate of return is 5.9% for 3 weeks, so if you were to average a 5.9% return every 4 weeks, you'd have an annual return of 71%. If you own stock and this is the first time you're learning about covered calls, shame on your stock broker (but don't worry, you're not alone). Think about the number of times over the life of the stock ownership that you could have benefited. You may be a lot closer to retiring if you had learned about covered calls years ago. With the help of this book, you will now have the ability to write covered calls on stocks that you own or stocks that you're willing to purchase.

Back to our example: because the current price of the stock is $74.69 and we chose to sell the $75 call option, we actually generated more premium than normal because at-the-money options are often over-priced, which is a perfect reason to sell the option.

In the next example (Figure 5.2), we'll sell the $80 call option for a mid-price of $2.45, which will allow us to increase our profit if the stock moves to $80 per share or higher. If the stock were to move above $80, we would be obligated to sell the stock at $80 a share. This would generate a profit of $5.31 per share ($74.69 cost of the stock minus the $80 selling price) and the call option premium of $2.45 per share for a total profit of $7.76. This would equal a 10.4% return for 3 weeks.

Again 10% per month multiplied by 12 months is an annual return of about 120%. The real difference between the 75 and 80 strike price is the strength of the stock; if you truly believe that the stock can move above 80, then sell the 80 strike price to maximize your investment return. If you're looking to be more conserva-

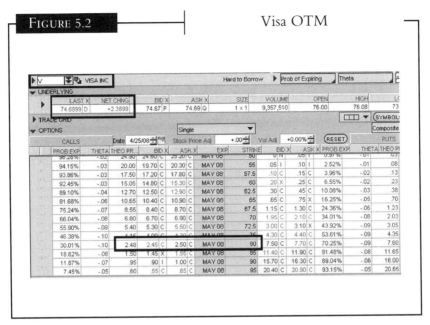

FIGURE 5.2 — Visa OTM

For color charts go to: www.traderslibrary.com/TLECorner • Chart by: thinkorswim.com

tive with increased odds of getting called out (selling your stock), then sell the $75 strike price. I personally prefer to be consistent, so I'd sell the closest option to the current stock price and if I was called out, I'd look to purchase the stock again and sell the call option next month.

Both of our examples for Visa met our requirement of selecting a strong stock; we had a $4.15 for the at-the-money option and a premium of $2.45 for the next out-of-the-money op-

INSIDER SECRET

It's important that you remember to look for financially and technically strong stocks because you'll need to buy the stock for a good month premium. One way to test the strength of the stock is to check the option premium before you purchase the stock. I've always made it a rule to not buy any stock that doesn't offer a minimum of at least one dollar premium per share for a four week time frame.

FIGURE 5.3 $75 Call Option
Probability of Expiring

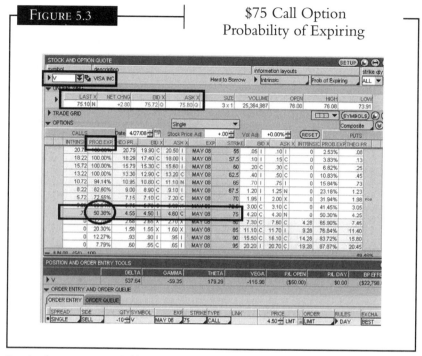

For color charts go to: www.traderslibrary.com/TLECorner • Chart by: thinkorswim.com

tion. This told us the stock had a good upside potential for the next three weeks.

We can use the probability of expiring to determine the odds of the stock moving above our strike price. Figure 5.3 shows that the 75 call option has a 50% probability of expiring, which tells us that we have a 50% chance of expiring in-the-money. So, the stock will have to close at $75 per share or above. Again, we have a 50% chance of keeping the entire option premium and selling the stock at $75 per share.

In our next example (Figure 5.4), the May $80 strike price has a probability of expiring of 32%. This tells us that the May $80 call option has a 32% chance of expiring in-the-money. Therefore, the

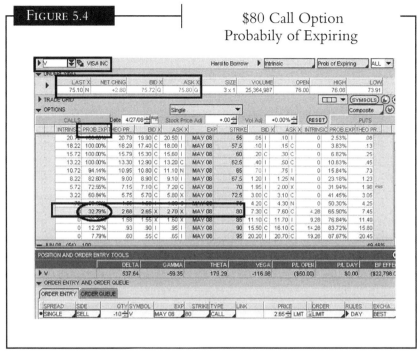

FIGURE 5.4

$80 Call Option
Probabily of Expiring

For color charts go to: www.traderslibrary.com/TLECorner • Chart by: thinkorswim.com

current stock price of $75.10 will have to increase to $80 or higher to be in-the-money.

GUIDELINES TO WRITING COVERED CALLS

Here are a couple of guidelines I like to look for when writing a covered call. First, a minimum monthly premium of $1.00 per share for the current month with one to three weeks before expiration and one strike price higher than the current price of the stock. This is often an option that is out-of-the-money one strike price (the next strike price is above the current price of stock). If the stock shows signs of weakness, you may want to buy back the option you sold to close out the trade. At this time your cost could be less than the premium you received or, in some cases, more if the stock increased in value since you wrote the covered call.

Timing is important; often once the MACD indicator has topped out and begins moving lower, you'll want to sell the call option to maximize your premium income before the stock drops because your call option premiums decrease in value as the stock drops in value. Looking at Figure 5.5, you'll see a chart for Caterpillar (CAT).

If you focus on the MACD indicator, you'll see it moving lower as the stock price does. By selling the call option now, instead of waiting, you'll bring in a larger credit than if you were to wait for the stock to drop more. Also, it is important to note that the stock price could not break up through its resistance level (ceiling), which

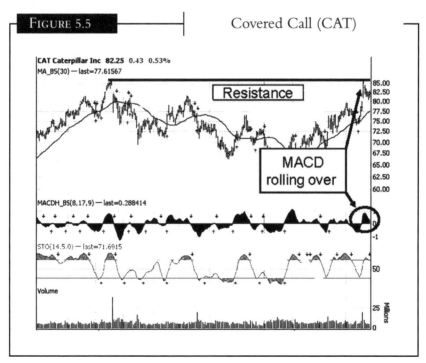

FIGURE 5.5 — Covered Call (CAT)

For color charts go to: www.traderslibrary.com/TLECorner • Chart by: thinkorswim.com

shows signs of weakness. At this time, I would be looking to sell the call option that is lower than the current price of the stock to increase the odds of selling the stock come expiration. With an increasing MACD indicator, I would be more bullish. Selling an out-of-the-money call option with a decreasing MACD indicator, I would sell an in-the-money call option to increase the odds of selling the stock if the stock price flattened out.

Self-test questions

---

1. When selling a covered call, which of the following is considered to be the aggressive strike price?

     A. In-the-Money
     B. At-the-Money
     C. Out-of-the-Money

2. Of the various strike prices you can sell, which option tends to have more implied volatility priced into the option?

     A. In-the-Money
     B. At-the-Money
     C. Out-of-the-Money

3. Option traders look at various Greeks when determining their investment choice; when writing a covered call, which one of the three would be more important than the other two?

     A. Delta
     B. Gamma
     C. Theta

4. When writing a covered call, which expiration month would normally be best?

     A. One month out
     B. Two months out
     C. Three months out

5. Once you have executed your order and sold the covered call on the stock you own, can you place a stop loss on the stock too?

    A. Yes

    B. No

    C. On stocks only but not indexes

6. In order to sell a covered call on a stock you own, the stock must be optionable and you can only sell the stock in groups of?

    A. 50 shares

    B. 75 shares

    C. 100 shares

7. If prior to your expiration date you chose to close out your covered call trade, you would need to execute which of the following orders to close the trade?

    A. Buy to close

    B. Sell to open

    C. Sell to close

8. True or False: Say you were to buy a stock at $73 per share and sold the $75 call option for the current month of May. Then 2 weeks before the May expiration, the stock was trading at $78 per share. The stock could be called away before the expiration in May.

    A. True

    B. False

9. If you own stock and are looking to continue ownership of the stock but technically see signs of weakness, which technical indictor would be best to determine that weakness and allow you to time your covered call?

    A. Moving Average
    B. MACD
    C. Stochastics

10. If your stock does show signs of weakness and you want to sell a covered call to generate a premium during the pull back, which strike price would you prefer to sell?

    A. In-the-Money
    B. At-the-Money
    C. Out-of-the-Money

For answers, go to www.traderslibrary.com/TLEcorner.

Six

Put It Down: Buying Put Options

IN THIS CHAPTER

Creating profit with put options
Guidelines for writing
Chart examples with low dollar and high dollar stocks

The purchase of put options can be a very rewarding way to make money in a bearish market but you need to remember that the stock or index you're selecting must move down in order for you to make money. This type of investment strategy works really well if you can identify stocks that are in weak groups, such as the housing group during the years 2005 through 2008 or even the banking/financial group, which took its share of abuse after selling sub-prime loans to investors who couldn't afford them years later when interest rates continued to increase.

Regardless of the reason why the group or stock is dropping, it is our objective to select the correct put option to purchase so when the stock drops in value, our investment increases in value. In order for you to understand how this works, don't overanalyze what I'm about to say. A put option can be either purchased or sold (in this case we'll be buying the put option), which would give us the right to sell our stock to someone at a higher price (chosen strike price) if the stock dropped. If you did own stock and purchased a put option, you could force the sale of your stock to someone such as in this example:

> **Purchased $50 put option at $3.00 per share.**
> **Stock dropped to $42 per share.**
>
> **You exercise your right to sell your $50 stock to someone at the $50 price when its real value is now $42. You avoided an $8 loss minus your $3 cost of the option:**
> **$50 - $42 = $8 - $3 = $5.**
> **In this example, you netted $5.**

You're pretty good if you understood this example on the first read because most investors don't. This is what is known as a protective put option. It is a strategy I don't encourage investors to do because

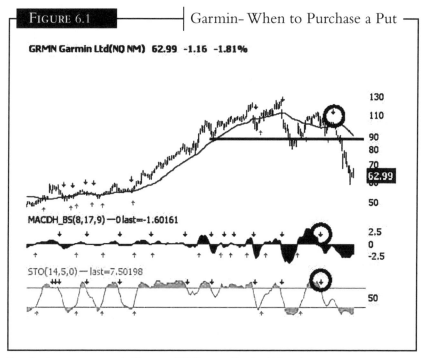

FIGURE 6.1 — Garmin- When to Purchase a Put

For color charts go to: www.traderslibrary.com/TLECorner • Chart by: thinkorswim.com

it's a way to limit your losses on a stock you own. My belief is if the stock is showing signs of weakness, then I'd rather sell the stock or place a stop loss to limit the downside losses.

Puts for Profit

Let's talk about why and how to buy a put option solely for the purpose of a profit. You choose a strike and look for the stock to drop below it. The further the stock drops below this strike price, the greater your profit will be. Let's begin with the chart of a stock which has a recent downtrend and bearish technical indictors. As you'll see within this Garmin chart (Figure 6.1), the stock had a nice bullish upward run; however, it reaches a price high of $120, then moves lower to a support level of $90. After that, it moves back up

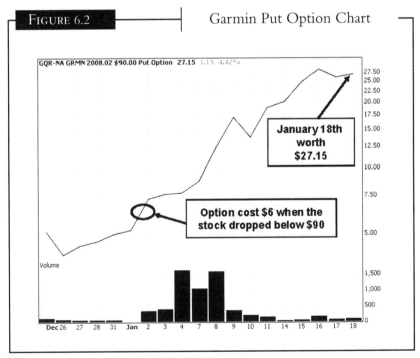

FIGURE 6.2 Garmin Put Option Chart

GQR-NA GRMN 2008.02 $90.00 Put Option 27.15 1.15 4.42%

January 18th worth $27.15

Option cost $6 when the stock dropped below $90

For color charts go to: www.traderslibrary.com/TLECorner • Chart by: thinkorswim.com

to $110 before finally breaking below the previous support level of $90 and continuing to $62.99, for about a 27 point drop. This is a good example of when to purchase a put option.

After viewing the chart of GRMN, look at the option chart to see exactly what the cost of the option was on December 26. You can also see what your cost would have been on January 2 when the price of the stock dropped below that all-important support level of $90 (Figure 6.2). Your put option cost was $6 per share, but again keep in mind that you can only trade options in groups of 100 shares (a contract). So, if you had an investment of $600 (the minimum investment) and you elected to sell the option on January 18th, then its value would be $27.15 per share equaling $2,715.00, or a 353% rate of return for less than one month's time.

This is exactly why an investor such as yourself should learn how to make money on weak stocks and bear markets. I get excited about trading a bear market more than a bull market because when stocks drop, they drop faster than they go up; this simply means you can make more money quicker.

Let's talk about your risk within this trade, because every investment in the stock market has a certain amount of risk. When you purchase a put option, your maximum risk is the $600 you spent to invest in one contract, and you'll lose the entire amount if the stock doesn't move below $90.

You need to learn how to make money on weak stocks and bear markets because when stocks drop, they drop faster than they go up; this simply means you can make more money quicker.

As a second example we're going to show you the put potential on an over-priced stock—Google. A quick look at Figure 6.3 and you'll see the stock has been weak and trending to the downside, and our technical indicators are showing signs of weakness.

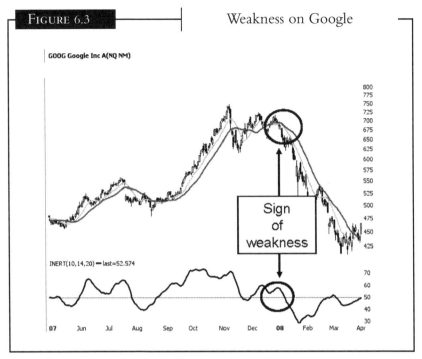

FIGURE 6.3 ———————————— Weakness on Google ——————

GOOG Google Inc A(NQ NM)

INERT(10,14,20) ◆ last=52.574

Sign of weakness

For color charts go to: www.traderslibrary.com/TLECorner • Chart by: thinkorswim.com

The March 680 put option cost $39.20 per share on January 3, 2008 (Figure 6.4). As of March 20, 2008, the 680 put option was trading at $226.60 per share as seen in Figure 6.5. This is an increase of $187.40 per share (or $18,740 per contract), equaling a 378% return for about 3 months. As with the purchase of a call option, these are not everyday trades, but if you're willing to risk a portion of your investment money, you could really hit some home runs.

The key to buying put options is to time the market; wait for a bear market and then look for industry groups that are over-priced. An example of an over-priced industry group at the time of writing would be the oil and metal groups. Stocks within these groups have seen prices that they have never seen before, but all stocks drop after a certain amount of time and when the industry falls out of favor the stocks within such groups, like the oil and metal groups,

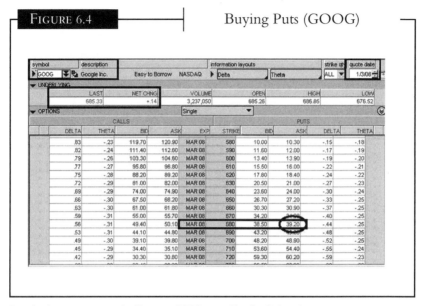

FIGURE 6.4 — Buying Puts (GOOG)

For color charts go to: www.traderslibrary.com/TLECorner • Chart by: thinkorswim.com

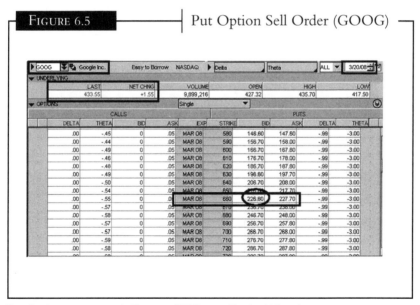

FIGURE 6.5 — Put Option Sell Order (GOOG)

For color charts go to: www.traderslibrary.com/TLECorner • Chart by: thinkorswim.com

will drop over 50% in value. Thinking back to the late '90s, it was the dot-com stocks such as eBay and Yahoo that were trading over $400 per share and then, starting in 2000, they dropped to the low $30 price range. After 2005, home builders such as Beazer Homes reached over $80 per share (stock split adjusted) and then by 2008 were trading at just $10 per share.

What goes up will always go down, so keep this in mind when searching for put option candidates and look for over-priced stocks within hot industry groups. Wait for signs of weakness and time your entry with the use of good technical indicators. If you believe that given plenty of time your stock of choice will drop, then stay away from a short term option and look into what are known as LEAPS. With these options both calls and puts can have up to 2 ½ years before expiration and even though they will be costly (because of the amount of time you're purchasing), they can really pay off. As

LINGO
Long-Term Equity Anticipation Securities (LEAPS)® are publicly traded options contracts with expiration dates that are longer than one year. LEAPS are not structurally different than short-term options, but they are useful for long term investors who want to take advantage of prolonged price changes. (Source: Investopedia.com)

with almost all options, you can sell the option any time before its expiration date.

Self-test questions

1. One looks to purchase put options on stocks that have greater odds of moving which direction?

    A. Up
    B. Down
    C. Sideways
    D. Down or Sideways

2. When selecting a put option to purchase, which option will give you a larger return on your investment as the stock drops?

    A. In-the-Money
    B. At-the-Money
    C. Out-of-the-Money

3. When buying put options, you can lose more than the original out of pocket investment.

    A. True
    B. False

4. You can purchase put options for which of the following purposes?

    A. You want to purchase the stock for a certain price.
    B. You're looking to sell your option for profit when the stock drops.
    C. You own the underlying stock and purchase a put option— giving you the right to sell the stock at that predetermined strike price if the stock drops in value.
    D. Both B and C

5. True or False: The purchase of a put option could benefit an investor if he/she owns the stock.

    A. True
    B. False

6. When purchasing a put option to benefit on a stock's move down, the option that would cost the least would be?

    A. In-the-Money
    B. At-the-Money
    C. Out-of-the-Money

7. If you were to purchase a put option with a strike price that is in-the-money, the stock price at the time of the option purchase would need to be?

    A. Higher than your strike price

    B. Lower than your strike price

8. What portion of your put option cost is more important?

    A. Intrinsic Value

    B. Extrinsic Value

    C. Retrinsic Value

9. To increase your profit potential when purchasing a put option, you would rather see which of the following?

    A. Downtrending stock

    B. Downtrending stock market

    C. Downtrending industry group

10. When selecting a stock to purchase a put option which of the following do I consider to the most important?

    A. Bad company financials

    B. The correct option

    C. Money moving out of the industry group

    D. The right technical signals

For answers, go to www.traderslibrary.com/TLEcorner.

Seven

Passing It On: Selling Puts

IN THIS CHAPTER

Rules for selling naked puts
Examining the role of theta
Closing the trade to mitigate risk

IF YOU'RE AN OWNER of stock, you'll want to pay very close attention to this chapter because I'm going to share with you what most brokerage firms fail to teach you. You can purchase stock at a discount.

SELLING A NAKED PUT OPTION

Selling a naked put option gives you the right to purchase the underlying stock at a set price on or before a set date. As with any successful trade, there are rules. Let's begin by outlining the two most important rules of this strategy and then I'll walk you through a couple of educational examples.

RULE NUMBER ONE

You must like the stock. This means you're willing to own the stock because someone has the right to make you purchase the stock on or before the selected expiration date, and depending on the market conditions, the stock could be dropping while you take ownership of the stock. It's important to keep in mind that this strategy is used because you're willing to purchase the stock; the only difference is you're looking to purchase it at a price lower than the current price.

RULE NUMBER TWO

You must be willing to own the stock at a certain price (strike price) on or before the chosen expiration date.

Now we also have a few requirements about the stock. First, the stock should have strong fundamentals, an upward trend, and the industry group should have been trending up for at least the past several weeks. Looking at Figure 7.1, you'll see our selected com-

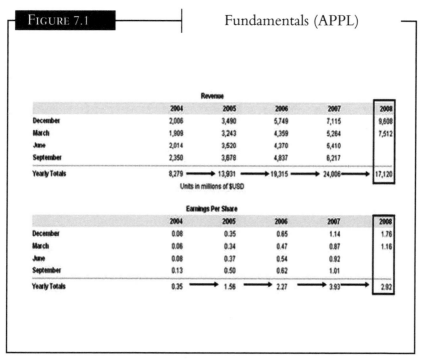

FIGURE 7.1   Fundamentals (APPL)

Revenue

	2004	2005	2006	2007	2008
December	2,006	3,490	5,749	7,115	9,608
March	1,909	3,243	4,359	5,264	7,512
June	2,014	3,520	4,370	5,410	
September	2,350	3,678	4,837	6,217	
Yearly Totals	8,279 →	13,931 →	19,315 →	24,006 →	17,120

Units in millions of $USD

Earnings Per Share

	2004	2005	2006	2007	2008
December	0.08	0.35	0.85	1.14	1.76
March	0.06	0.34	0.47	0.87	1.16
June	0.08	0.37	0.54	0.92	
September	0.13	0.50	0.62	1.01	
Yearly Totals	0.35 →	1.56 →	2.27 →	3.93 →	2.92

For color charts go to: www.traderslibrary.com/TLECorner • Chart by: thinkorswim.com

pany has increasing revenue and earnings per share year over year. Looking at the far right of the chart, you'll see that the 2008 Revenue and Earnings Per Share information for the months June and September have not been released at time of writing.

As you would with any company, you'll look to see that the revenue and earnings that have been released for the recent year exceed the revenue and earnings for the months of December and March of the most recent past year, in this case 2007. The revenue for December 2007 was 7,115 and in 2008, it grew to 9,608. Doing the same for March, you'll see an increase from 5,264 in 2007 to 7,512 in 2008. The earnings per share for the months of December and March 2008 exceed the earnings per share for the months of December and March 2007—exactly what you want to see.

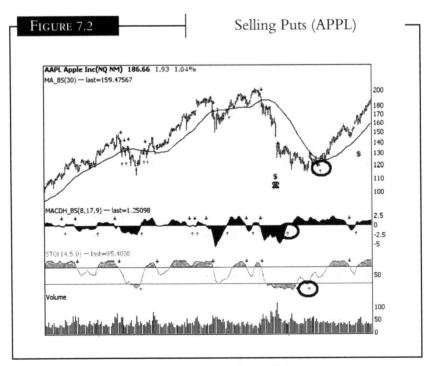

FIGURE 7.2 — Selling Puts (APPL)

For color charts go to: www.traderslibrary.com/TLECorner • Chart by: thinkorswim.com

In the second example (Figure 7.2) you'll see that AAPL bottomed out at about $120 per share, with a buy opportunity being shown. The technical indicator arrows show an entry point at the $130 price as the stock moved above its short-term resistance (ceiling).

The industry group is also in an uptrend (Figure 7.3). Let's say that you are still willing to purchase the Apple stock. Its current price is $186.66, so the purchase of the 1,000 shares would be $186,660. Now look at Figure 7.4 to see an example of selling a naked put option instead of buying the stock.

Beginning with Section A, you'll see the current price of the stock is $186.66 per share. As you move down to Section B, you'll see that the sale of the May 180 put option is priced at $2.18 per share; so, selling the May 180 put option for 10 contracts will generate

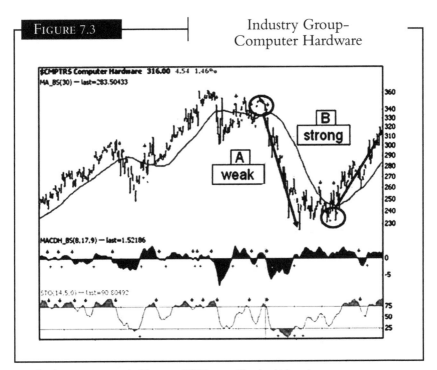

FIGURE 7.3 — Industry Group– Computer Hardware

For color charts go to: www.traderslibrary.com/TLECorner • Chart by: thinkorswim.com

$2,180 cash into your account. The margin requirement for this trade is about 20% of the stock's current price, which is $37,332. All of this adds up to a 6% return for 7 trading days.

Now keep in mind the two very important rules for selling naked put options; you must be willing to buy the stock and you must be willing to buy it at the strike price you sold. In this example we sold the $180 strike price while the stock was trading at $186.66, and we received $2.18 per share. If and only if the stock closes below the 180 strike price on the expiration date (third Friday of May) would we be forced to sell the stock over the weekend, which would give us a cost of $177.82 ($180 minus the $2.18 premium we received).

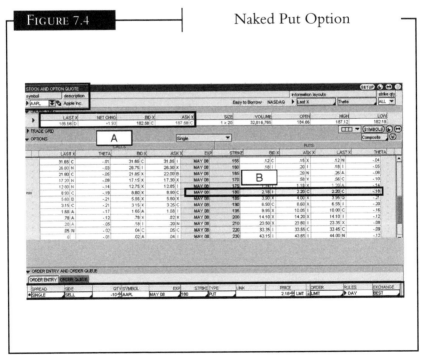

FIGURE 7.4   Naked Put Option

For color charts go to: www.traderslibrary.com/TLECorner • Chart by: thinkorswim.com

At this point you have to be asking yourself: does this have greater risk than just buying the stock at its current price? No, you can either buy the stock at $186.66 per share or $177.82 per share. If the stock doesn't close below the $180 price, you can't purchase the stock; however, you do keep the $2.18 per share, or $2,180 for 10 contracts.

This is a win–win situation because you make money on a stock that you'd like to buy but don't have to own. Your risk is actually the upside potential of the stock because if you purchased the stock at $186.66 and it kept moving higher, you'd make more.

NAKED PUT TRADE EXAMPLE

Let's walk through an example of a naked put trade, beginning with the trade confirmation seen in Figure 7.5.

Starting with the bottom of the confirmation slip, you'll see that we were filled at a price of $2.60 per share. Based on our 10-contract trade, we received $2,600 into our account. Looking in the middle of the confirmation slip, you'll see that the current price at the close of the day was $1.65 per share, which means that our profit for the day was $.95 or $950 (.95 x 1,000) if we closed out the trade. Since we have not closed out the trade, it's not a profit yet.

Profits should only be accounted for when the trade has closed because even in this case the stock could drop below our strike price and create a loss instead of a profit.

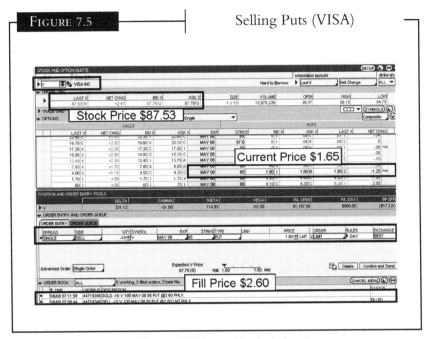

For color charts go to: www.traderslibrary.com/TLECorner • Chart by: thinkorswim.com

This trade is considered to be aggressive. Let me explain. We sold the May $85 put option for a premium of $2.60 and at the time of the trade, the stock price was at $85.47. By the end of the day, the stock closed at $87.53 per share. Our goal is for the stock to remain above our $85 naked put price on expiration Friday, which for this trade is seven trading days away. If the stock closes below the $85 strike price, we will own 1,000 shares at the $85 price minus the $2.60 premium, giving us a cost base of $82.40 per share. The more conservative trade would be to sell the $80 put option for a premium of $.90 per share. In this case, you would look for the stock to remain above $80 and your profit would be $900 (10 contracts over 7 trading days).

THE THETA ADVANTAGE

The point of selling any option is to take advantage of the theta, which is the time decay portion of an option. The theta for this option is $.11 per day as seen in Figure 7.6. As each day passes, we'll receive $180 of profit because we sold an option that offered $.11 of theta per share. Based on the 10 days before expiration, it's about $110 per day. As the expiration date gets closer, the option premium will drop even more because the odds of the stock closing below the $85 price have decreased. With this type of investment strategy, I can be wrong and still make money. The stock can go up and I keep the $2,600; it can go sideways and I keep the $2,600; and it can even go down to $85 and I keep the $2,600. The only time I lose any money on this trade is when the stock drops below $82.40 and if that were to happen, I'm still in control because I can either close the naked put trade and avoid having the stock put to me or take ownership of the stock for $82.40 per share instead of the $85 per share. At this time I can hold on to the stock until it moves higher and sell the stock or write a covered call (covered in chapter four)

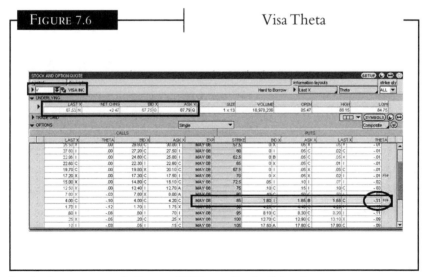

FIGURE 7.6   Visa Theta

For color charts go to: www.traderslibrary.com/TLECorner • Chart by: thinkorswim.com

bringing in a premium for the next month while giving someone the right to buy the stock from me.

How to Close the Trade

Let's talk about the "what if" situation and say the stock dropped below $82.40 per share before the expiration date. If you no longer want to allow the stock to be put to you at $85 per share, you would close out the trade by executing a buy to close order. This could leave you with a profit but in some cases if the stock really moved below your break even price of $82.40, it could cost you more than the premium you received. But, if you no longer like the stock, it's still best to close out the trade and avoid having to purchase the stock.

Figure 7.7 shows an order to close the trade; take a look and become familiar with the process in case you elect to close out of a trade before expiration. Keep in mind a good trader will set an order to "buy to close" at a limit price and when the option trades at that price, then your order will be closed.

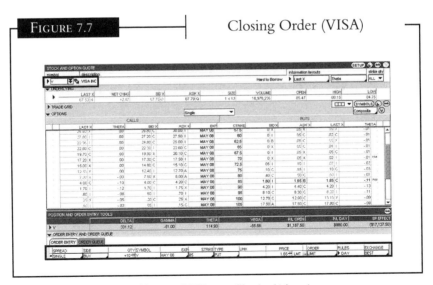

FIGURE 7.7 Closing Order (VISA)

For color charts go to: www.traderslibrary.com/TLECorner • Chart by: thinkorswim.com

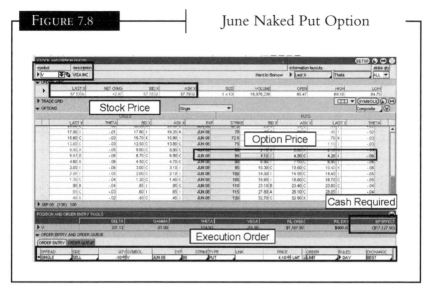

FIGURE 7.8 June Naked Put Option

For color charts go to: www.traderslibrary.com/TLECorner • Chart by: thinkorswim.com

For example, I have been selling naked puts on Visa for several months during its bullish move up. Once I entered the trade, I set an order to "buy to close" for a limit price of $.10. When the option premium erodes away as the stock moves higher and time passes, my option will be automatically closed at the $.10, and I can free up my cash and move on to another trade.

In our last example of Visa (Figure 7.8), we will examine a June option that is about 45 days before the June expiration date. Looking at Figure 7.8 this trade will give us a $4.10 premium for the June $85 put option. Based on this example we'll make $4.50 for 45 days if the stock remains above $85 (at this time it's at $87.53). With a cash requirement of $17,127.50, our rate of return will be a nice 24%.*

---

* Margin requests for naked put trades vary with brokerage firms, a normal requirement would be about 20% of the current stock's premium plus the credit received for the trade.

If, however, the stock was to drop below $85 and you were to take ownership of the stock, your choices would be to hold onto the stock and let it increase to your desired sale price, which could be any price above your cost base of $80.90, or to write a covered call for the following month once the stock is assigned to you.

Self-test questions

1. When selling a naked put option, you must follow two very important rules. Which of the three is not one of these rules?

   A. Must be willing to own the stock.

   B. Never sell a put option with less than two weeks of time.

   C. Be willing to own the stock at the selected strike price you sold.

2. The option Greek that is most important when selling naked put options is:

   A. Gamma

   B. Beta

   C. Theta

   D. Delta

3. The term selling naked put options means?

   A. You place the trade when you have don't have clothes on.

   B. Your upside risk is unlimited.

   C. You sold something you don't own.

4. When selling naked put options you prefer that the stock moves?

   A. Up

   B. Down

   C. Sideways

   D. All of the above

5. The sale of a naked put option gives someone the right to?

    A. Buy the stock from you
    B. Sell the stock to you
    C. Both

6. When selling naked put options, which of the following would be your margin (cash requirement) for the trade?

    A. 20 percent
    B. 30 percent
    C. 50 percent

7. If you were really bullish and wanted to benefit during an upward movement of a stock, which option strike price would you sell?

    A. Out-of-the-Money
    B. At-the-Money
    C. In-the-Money

8. What is the worst thing a naked put option investor could do when selling a put option?

    A. Not close the trade early for a profit
    B. Allow the stock to be put to them
    C. Panic

9. If you sold a naked put option and the stock was below your selected strike price come expiration day, it would be important to check which of the following to determine if you would allow the stock to be put to you?

    A. The support and resistance level of the stock
    B. The direction of the industry group the stock is in
    C. The covered call premium for the following month

10. Taking a worst case example, say you sold the June $80 naked put option and come the third Friday before the stock market closed, the stock was trading at $75 per share and you received $3 per share for the option; what could you do?

    A. Nothing and have the stock put to you.

    B. Close out the trade by purchasing the same strike price for the same month to avoid having the stock put (sold) to you at the selected strike price.

    C. Close out the trade and place another one for the next month if you believe the stock will move higher.

    D. All of the above

For answers, go to www.traderslibrary.com/TLEcorner.

Eight

Spreading the Wealth: Vertical Bull Put Spreads

IN THIS CHAPTER

Determining a vertical bull put spread
Conservative and aggressive trade examples
Building a base for more advanced strategies

A VERTICAL CALL SPREAD is two vertical put options, created by selling a higher put option and buying a lower put option, and thereby creating a credit. The best candidates for a vertical put spread would be bullish stocks that have the ability to move higher. Using the company Apple Computer, I'll show you the results of a bull put vertical spread.

I write a weekly report for www.incometrader.com and this is a sample report taken from there. It shows a detailed trade with a 19% return for 1 week. I'm using this example to show you how important it is to select the right investment strategy based on your risk.

This type of a trade is done within the "stay rich" bag of money, so even though the stock was bullish with strong financials, up and coming annual MacWorld conference, and earnings to be released in a week, we took the safe trade instead of buying call options (which would only benefit us if the stock went up). Because the stock actually dropped from $172 to $161, we still made 19% for the week on a bullish strategy.

Let's review the report and then we'll come back and cover the details of the spread trade and, more important, the risk versus the reward. We'll also discuss how to save the trade if you're wrong (a section that many forget to cover in their options books) and if you do it correctly, make more than the 19%. Being wrong about a trade and still making money? Now, that's why knowledge is priceless.

INCOMETRADER REPORT: VERTICAL BULL PUT SPREAD

We refer to this as a vertical spread because we sell the higher strike price and buy the lower strike price. In this example, we sold the $160 put option and bought the $155 put option for a net credit of $.80 per share, or $800 for 10 contracts. The goal is for the stock to remain above the $160 price come this Friday expiration, which is one week from today.

When the stock closes above the $160 price (support level), we will reach the maximum profit potential of $800 with a cash requirement (money in your account) of $4,200, giving us a rate of return of 19% for 1 week. This trade is attractive because Apple has its annual MAC World conference beginning on Monday. Earnings will be released on the Tuesday following this Friday's expiration, which allows us to be out of the trade during the release of their earnings just in case the stock drops.

HOW DID WE DETERMINE OUR TRADE?

If you look at the first chart for AAPL (Figure 8.1), you'll see that the stock was showing signs of weakness after reaching the $200 price (resistance) and then it dropped below the 30-day moving average. By reading the chart first, we were able to determine that if

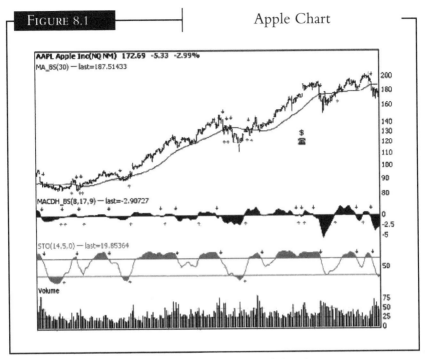

FIGURE 8.1 ⟶ Apple Chart

For color charts go to: www.traderslibrary.com/TLECorner • Chart by: thinkorswim.com

the stock did continue to drop, it should find a support level at the $160 price, which was its previous low.

If you look at two other technical indicators (MACD and Stochastics), you'll notice that they too were showing downside weakness. Both were trending downward after the stock reached the $200 price.

The second chart of APPL (Figure 8.2) shows the stock closing at $161.36, which is just above our $160 support level. Even more important, it is above our $160 strike price, which is what we need in order for both options to expire and for us to be profitable with the bull put spread trade.

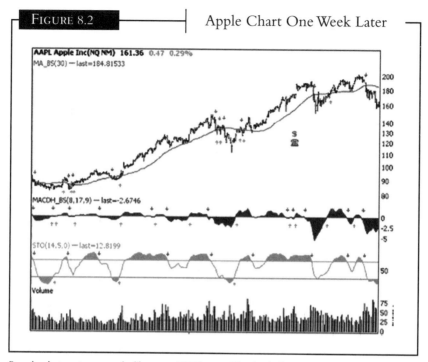

FIGURE 8.2 — Apple Chart One Week Later

For color charts go to: www.traderslibrary.com/TLECorner • Chart by: thinkorswim.com

BULL PUT SPREAD TRADE- SPECIFIC EXAMPLES

I'm going to take a few minutes and use several charts to break down the details of a bull put spread because this may just be the one strategy that you focus on within your "stay rich" brokerage account, but before I do so, I need you to take a deep breath and clear your mind. In chapter six we discussed buying a put option for bearish markets and stocks and in chapter seven we covered selling naked put options on bullish stocks you'd be willing to own.

Close your eyes for a second before reading on and do not think outside of what you're reading. Trust me, you'll have a better understanding of this strategy and even how to place the trade within seconds.

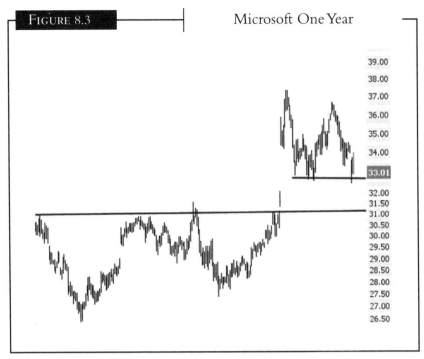

CONSERVATIVE STOCK TRADE

The first chart we're going to view is Microsoft, which is a very slow-moving conservative stock that offers less risk than our second stock, Google. By using these two completely different stocks you'll be able to see that bull put spreads can work on any stock regardless of the price of the stock.

Let's begin by having you view the one year chart of Microsoft (MSFT) so that we can determine its area of support. Then, we'll put together two different put option strike prices for the same stock with the same expiration month giving us the bull put vertical spread.

FIGURE 8.4		Vertical Bull Spread Prices			
15 / 17.5	-.01	.01	.00	0
17.5 / 20	-.01	.02	.00	0
20 / 22.5	-.01	.02	.00	0
22.5 / 25	.01	.03	.00	-.01
25 / 27.5	.09	.11	-.01	0
27.5 / 30	.27	.31	-.01	-.02
30 / 32.5	.72	.77	-.01	-.02
32.5 / 35	1.40	1.44	.00	-.01
35 / 37.5	1.95	2.12	.01	+.05
37.5 / 40	2.25	2.50	.00	-.35

For color charts go to: www.traderslibrary.com/TLECorner • Chart by: thinkorswim.com

The most important part of placing this spread trade is to determine the most recent area of support for the stock. In this case (Figure 8.3), it is the $33 price where I've drawn a line. The next level of support is the $31 price. This price was resistance when the stock was moving up (old resistance becomes new support).

The most important part of placing a spread trade is determining the most recent areas of support and resistance.

Now that we know that the next lowest support level is about $31, we want to choose a strike price that is below this level of support because our goal is for the stock to be above our strike price come expiration day.

To keep the process simple, I'm going to select a vertical spread from my online trading account (thinkorswim.com) and see what the current spread premium is if I were to sell the $30 strike price and buy the $27.50 strike price (Figure 8.4). You'll see that the lower price (the bid price) is $.27 per share and the higher price (the ask price) is $.31 per share.

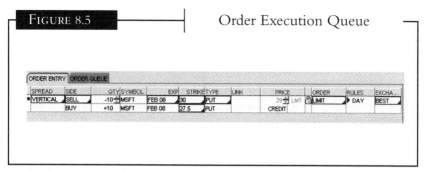

FIGURE 8.5 | Order Execution Queue

For color charts go to: www.traderslibrary.com/TLECorner • Chart by: thinkorswim.com

By left clicking your mouse on the bid price of $.27, it will load the order and complete both parts of the trade with one click. The current bid price for the $27.50/$30 spread is $.27, which is quoted per share. Say we place a trade for 10 contracts; we would bring into our account $270 ($.27 x 1,000 shares) for a four-week trade (expiration is the third Friday of the week). Our goal is for the stock to remain above the $30 strike price. Then, the options will expire worthless and give us a 12% return for four weeks.

If you closed your eyes like I asked earlier, you should have a better understanding of how we placed a vertical put spread on Microsoft.

INSIDER SECRET

The actual bid price is $.27 per share; however, once you click on that bid price of $.27, the execution platform (Order Queue in Figure 8.5) will give you a credit price of $.29 per share, giving you an extra $.2 per share, which equals another $20 for the trade and a 13% return instead of a 12% return. This occurs because your order is routed to the different exchanges to get you the best price and allowing us retail traders to benefit from the various prices offered. Please keep in mind that it could take a few minutes to get the better price; so, if you need your order executed quickly, then adjust your price to $.27 and you'll be filled within seconds.

But just in case you didn't, let's review what happened.

- Our first step was to determine if the stock was bullish (trending upwards) in the last several months.

- Then, we selected our shorter-term support level of $33 and the longer-term support level of $31.

- We chose to sell the current month put option strike price of $30 (no more than 4 weeks from expiration) and purchase the current month put option strike price of $27.50.

- This gave us a credit of $.27 per share based on the bid price or if using thinkorswim, $.29 per share.

- Our 4.1% rate of return based on the $.29 credit is $290 divided by $2,210, which is the difference between the $30 strike price and the $27.50 strike price. This equals a maximum loss of no more than $2,210 and that would only be if the stock closed below the lower strike price of $27.50.

Remember, we sell on the bid price and buy on the ask price. Also, you must have $2,210 cash in your account to place the trade and you cannot lose any more than this amount even if the stock goes to zero.

AGGRESSIVE STOCK TRADE

Now, let's look at our second example (Figure 8.6) and see what type of risk and reward we could get from the $600 stock Google. As with the Microsoft example, we must first begin with a chart and determine our short-term and long-term support level. In this example, we chose the $600 price as the short-term support level because the stock actually closed above $600. It is a strong sign of support when this occurs at an even number such as $600, $500, etc. Our real concern is not the short-term support level of $600; it's the long-term support level, which was the past resistance level of $560 (Figure 8.6). If you look at the chart, you'll see that the stock tried to move higher but couldn't and ended up dropping back towards the $475 price.

Now, knowing the stock can drop to about $560 per share, our rule is to select a strike price below this level of support ($560), which can be one of several choices. This time instead of just placing a vertical spread, like we did with Microsoft, I'm going to show you why a vertical bull put spread is safer, how the two different strike prices make up the spread trade, and more important, how the spread reduces our risk even with a $600 stock.

We will buy the lower strike price and then sell the higher strike price, giving us a net credit difference between what we spend for

FIGURE 8.6 — Google One Year

For color charts go to: www.traderslibrary.com/TLECorner • Chart by: thinkorswim.com

the lower strike price and what we receive for selling the higher strike price. Now, there are several different strike prices that let you place various spreads, but I'm looking for a consistent rate of return within my "stay rich" account.

Knowing that the support level is the $560 price and stock was currently trading at $600, I would choose the $530/$520 vertical bull put spread, which means I'm bullish and I want the stock to remain above $530 per share come expiration four weeks from now.

Many brokerage firms don't have the ability to place both of the trades at the same time; so, I'll walk you through the process of placing one first (buy the $520, Figure 8.7) and then the second (sell the $530, Figure 8.8). This must be done in this order. If you sell the options first ($530 strike price), you've sold a naked put option,

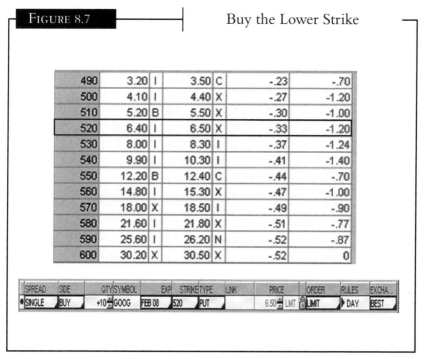

FIGURE 8.7   Buy the Lower Strike

490	3.20	I	3.50	C	-.23	-.70
500	4.10	I	4.40	X	-.27	-1.20
510	5.20	B	5.50	X	-.30	-1.00
520	6.40	I	6.50	X	-.33	-1.20
530	8.00	I	8.30	I	-.37	-1.24
540	9.90	I	10.30	I	-.41	-1.40
550	12.20	B	12.40	C	-.44	-.70
560	14.80	I	15.30	X	-.47	-1.00
570	18.00	X	18.50	I	-.49	-.90
580	21.60	I	21.80	X	-.51	-.77
590	25.60	I	26.20	N	-.52	-.87
600	30.20	X	30.50	X	-.52	0

SPREAD	SIDE	QTY	SYMBOL	EXP	STRIKE	TYPE	LNK	PRICE	ORDER	RULES	EXCHA...
•SINGLE	BUY	+10	GOOG	FEB 08	520	PUT		6.50 LMT	LIMIT	DAY	BEST

For color charts go to: www.traderslibrary.com/TLECorner • Chart by: thinkorswim.com

which will require a minimum of 20% of the stock's current price. If this happens, your cash requirement will be $12,000 until you buy the $520 option. Then, your cash requirement will be the difference between the $530 and $520 strike price minus the cash credit you received, which leaves an amount of $8,300.

It's not just the difference between the cash requirement that's important; it's the risk that is unlimited if the stock really drops. Let's recap what you'll need to do. You buy (ask price) the lower of the two strike prices and then sell (bid price) the higher of the two strike prices, giving you the net credit. If you'll refer to Figure 8.9, you'll see we chose to use the vertical tab, which gave us the ability to buy and sell the two strike prices at the same time and create the credit of $1.70 (or $1,700 for 10 contracts). Again, when using a good brokerage firm, you'll be able to place your orders at the mid-price.

To determine our rate of return, we take the difference between the $530 and $520 price, which is $10 and subtract our credit of $1.70. This leaves a cash requirement of $8.30. Divide that by the credit of $1.70 and our rate of return is 20% for one month, but even more important, the stock can drop from $600 per share to $530 and we will still make 20%. Actually, the stock can go up, down (to $530), or even sideways and we still can make 20% for the month.

> **LINGO**
>
> **Mid-price** is a price in between the bid and ask prices. In this example, the bid price is $1.50 and the ask price is $1.90 for the $520/$530 strike price.

Rate of Return

Take the difference between the options: 530-520 = 10
Subtract the credit: 10- 1.70 = 8.30
Divide by the credit and multiply by 100 for a percentage:
8.30/1.70 x 100 = 20%

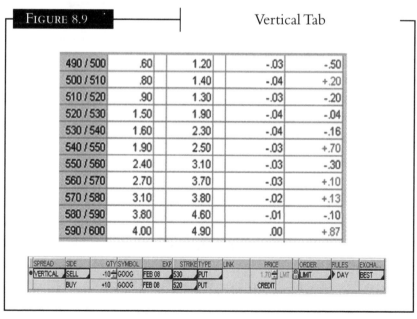

FIGURE 8.8 ─── | Sell the Higher Strike

490	3.20	I	3.50	C	-.23	-.70
500	4.10	I	4.40	X	-.27	-1.20
510	5.20	B	5.50	X	-.30	-1.00
520	6.40	I	6.50	X	-.33	-1.20
530	8.00	I	8.30	I	-.37	-1.24
540	9.90	I	10.30	I	-.41	-1.40
550	12.20	B	12.40	C	-.44	-.70
560	14.80	I	15.30	X	-.47	-1.00
570	18.00	X	18.50	I	-.49	-.90
580	21.60	I	21.80	X	-.51	-.77
590	25.60	I	26.20	N	-.52	-.87
600	30.20	X	30.50	X	-.52	0

SPREAD	SIDE	QTY	SYMBOL	EXP	STRIKE	TYPE	LINK	PRICE	ORDER	RULES	EXCHA...
• SINGLE	SELL	-10	GOOG	FEB 08	530	PUT		8.00 LMT	LIMIT	DAY	BEST

For color charts go to: www.traderslibrary.com/TLECorner • Chart by: thinkorswim.com

FIGURE 8.9 ─── | Vertical Tab

490 / 500	.60	1.20	-.03	-.50
500 / 510	.80	1.40	-.04	+.20
510 / 520	.90	1.30	-.03	-.20
520 / 530	1.50	1.90	-.04	-.04
530 / 540	1.60	2.30	-.04	-.16
540 / 550	1.90	2.50	-.03	+.70
550 / 560	2.40	3.10	-.03	-.30
560 / 570	2.70	3.70	-.03	+.10
570 / 580	3.10	3.80	-.02	+.13
580 / 590	3.80	4.60	-.01	-.10
590 / 600	4.00	4.90	.00	+.87

SPREAD	SIDE	QTY	SYMBOL	EXP	STRIKE	TYPE	LINK	PRICE	ORDER	RULES	EXCHA...
• VERTICAL	SELL	-10	GOOG	FEB 08	530	PUT		1.70 LMT	LIMIT	DAY	BEST
	BUY	+10	GOOG	FEB 08	520	PUT		CREDIT			

For color charts go to: www.traderslibrary.com/TLECorner • Chart by: thinkorswim.com

This is a perfect example of why it's better to sell the time premium of an option. If we bought the call options, we would pay for time premium and have to be in a trade where the stock must go up or we would risk a total loss of investment.

EXITING VERTICAL PUT SPREADS

The final thought about vertical put spreads is that they are an approved investment strategy for your self-directed retirement accounts, along with all the other various spread trades. Once you have practiced the trade with single contracts and perfected your skill, you may consider trading 10 contracts and building your retirement account because you will have the ability to defer your taxes until later years. But, you will have to learn how to exit the bull put spread if the stock shows great signs of weakness and is going to drop in value.

If this happened with Google, you would need to buy back the higher strike price ($530) for the current price (which often will be more than what you received when you sold the option) and keep the lower strike price ($520) put option, which will increase in value as the stock drops. When you decide to close out (it must be before the expiration date), you can sell the $520 put option for more than what you purchased it for. This option will only increase when the stock really begins to drop.

You must keep in mind that your decision to place the trade was based on the support level. Choosing the correct strike price below support is important because no matter how far the stock price drops, your trade will be 100% profitable unless it drops below the higher strike price of $530, which in this case would be 70 points away from the current stock price of $600.

This type of trade is based on time, meaning we're selling the time premium of an option and we want theta to melt away each day we get closer to our expiration date. Take a few minutes and review the question and answer section and see how well you have been able to comprehend the concept of a vertical bull put spread.

Once you master bull put spreads, then you'll want to move onto iron condor spreads, which is chapter 10. With this strategy you'll learn how to increase your rate of return and profit potential without increasing your risk. Doesn't that sound great? Increasing your rate of return but not your risk! Remember, you must first be good at vertical bull put spreads, then you can fully leverage the iron condor spreads.

Self-test questions

1. When placing a vertical bull put spread, our maximum profit is obtained if the price of the stock goes?

   A. Up
   B. Down
   C. Sideways
   D. All of the above

2. When placing this spread trade, you will need to view the stock chart to determine?

   A. Resistance
   B. Support
   C. Current Trend

3. How much cash is required to place a bull put spread trade?

   A. 20% of the stock price
   B. Difference between the two spread strike prices
   C. Difference between the two strike prices minus the credit received

4. If my broker doesn't offer the ability to place both trades at the same time, then I must place which trade first?

   A. Sell the higher strike price
   B. Buy the lower strike price

5. Of the three choices, which expiration month is best?

    A. One month expiration

    B. Two month expiration

    C. Three month expiration

    D. Doesn't matter, any of the above

6. Of the option Greeks, which one works to our advantage when placing a spread trade?

    A. Gamma

    B. Delta

    C. Theta

    D. Beta

7. When considering a stock for a bull put vertical spread, what should I avoid?

    A. Bad industry group

    B. Downtrending stock

    C. Earnings release date

    D. Break of short-term support

8. True or False: When placing the trade, you can adjust the execution order price between the bid and ask price to increase your credit.

    A. True

    B. False

9. Let's say you're really bullish on a stock and within the next 30 days before expiration you believe it has great upside potential. The stock is currently trading at $79 per share. Which of the four spreads would you select?

    A. $85/$90
    B. $80/$85
    C. $75/$80
    D. $70/$75

10. If I had to exit my spread earlier because the stock was dropping a lot in value, which choice would be best?

    A. Do nothing
    B. Buy back the higher strike price
    C. Sell the lower strike price
    D. Close out both sides of the trade at the same time

For answers, go to www.traderslibrary.com/TLEcorner.

Nine

What's the Spread: Vertical Bear Call Spreads

IN THIS CHAPTER

Examining the chart for high probability trades
Understanding risk and reward on vertical bear call spreads
Increasing profitability by looking for new trades

MANY OF THE ADVANCED option strategy names are somewhat self-explanatory, a bear call spread refers to being bearish; buying and selling a call option, creating a spread and limiting your risk. Often one would place a bear call spread in anticipation of a lower move during the next two to four weeks. The proper way to execute the bearish spread would be to buy and sell your selected options while at the same time create a credit spread and avoid placing yourself in a naked position (if you sold the call option without purchasing another call option).

Let's get to the visual part of the spread by viewing the charts and looking at the spread premiums. We'll then finalize the strategy with what I refer to as the "what if" situations; meaning what if the stock went up instead of down, what are my choices to avoid the maximum risk, or how can I take a losing trade and turn it into a winning trade?

REVIEWING THE CHART

The process of a vertical spread starts with the chart; you must have a good understanding of what is bullish and what is bearish and you must be able to identify the stock's major resistance level. As you'll see in Figure 9.1, Deere (DE) has established a major resistance level at the $95 price range; so, we'll place the vertical spread based on the fact that we want the stock to remain below the $95 price. This can be considered an aggressive spread with the stock trading at $89.53 per share.

Selling the May $95 strike price and buying the May $100 strike price (Figure 9.2) gives us a net credit of $1,000. Based upon a 10 contract trade, our risk would be $5,000 (difference between the $95 strike price and the $100 strike price). Then, if we subtract the

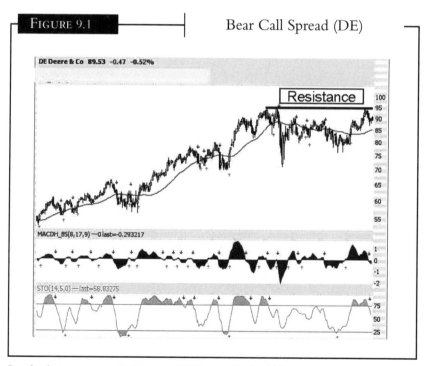

FIGURE 9.1 | Bear Call Spread (DE)

DE Deere & Co 89.53 -0.47 -0.52%

Resistance

MACDH_BS(8,17,9) —0 last=-0.293217

STO(14,5,0) — last=58.83275

For color charts go to: www.traderslibrary.com/TLECorner • Chart by: thinkorswim.com

$1,000 credit, it equals a maximum risk of $4,000. Your rate of re-turn is 20% for 3 weeks, and as long as the stock remains below the $95 strike price, your options will expire and give you the $1,000 maximum profit.

CLOSE THE OPTION YOU SOLD

It is a good habit to always close out the option you sold ($95 strike) to assure yourself that the stock doesn't turn bullish between the market close on Friday and the true expiration time of noon Saturday.

Let's say that on the third Friday of May (expiration day) the stock closed at $94.50, which is below our $95 strike price. You assume

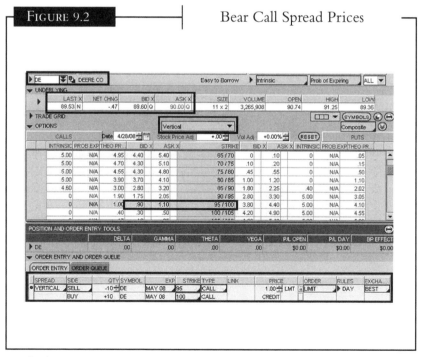

FIGURE 9.2 Bear Call Spread Prices

For color charts go to: www.traderslibrary.com/TLECorner • Chart by: thinkorswim.com

that the stock is not going above the $95 price, which is normally a safe way to think. But, what if after the close of the market on Friday, the company released some type of news and the after hours trading pushed the stock higher to $97 per share?

You now have a losing trade instead of a winning trade and your loss will be the difference between the current stock price of $97 and the $95 option you sold, which, in this example, equals a $2,000 loss minus the $1,000 credit maximum loss or $1,000 total. Please keep in mind that all brokerage firms are different and in some cases when the spread closes between your strike prices (between $95 and $100), you could be put the stock over the weekend and if it moves higher, your loss will increase.

Make it a habit to close out the short side (the option you sold) of the trade to be safe. This example is a three week trade and I've found it best to go no further out than 30 days to limit the risk of the stock moving up above the chosen strike price. As a safety precaution you can close out the trade anytime before the expiration and take the profit even if it's not the full $1 credit. Once I have entered the trade, I've found it to be helpful to place an order to close out the lower leg (lower strike price) for a limit price of $.10 so that when the spread trades at $.10, my order will be executed and will close out automatically.

As for the upper leg (higher strike price), you don't have to worry about closing it because you're long the call option and not short; so, you have no risk other than the price you paid for the option. If you do close out the lower strike price, you can keep the higher strike price and if the stock moves up, you can sell the option any time before expiration and increase your profit if it moves above the higher strike price.

CAUTION

I know that reading this can be very confusing no matter how easy I try to make it; so, please practice this until you truly know what you're doing. When you begin using real money, I would suggest that you start with a single contract for several months, then work your way up to ten contracts once you're comfortable with the strategy and how to exit the trade if you need to before expiration day. Another great way to begin would be to trade the higher strike price; although it will offer less of a credit, it will also have less risk.

Examine the Risk/Reward for Each Trade

Figure 9.3 shows you the $100/$105 bear vertical call spread. Looking at the bid price, you'll see that the credit (bottom of the chart) is $.40 per share equaling $400 for 10 contracts. Our risk is $4,600 with an 8.7% return for three weeks. Of course, the $95/$100 bear call spread with a $1,000 profit looks better, but the risk is higher. If you're new to options trading and looking for a conservative bearish investment strategy, an $8.7% three-week return is wonderful. If you multiplied that by 12 months, you would have an annual return of 104%.

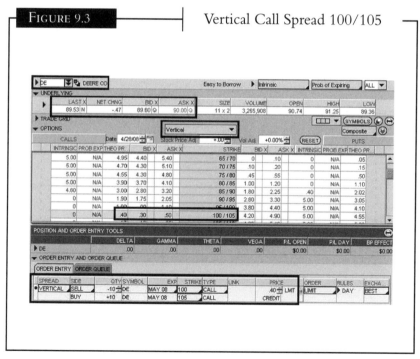

FIGURE 9.3 Vertical Call Spread 100/105

For color charts go to: www.traderslibrary.com/TLECorner • Chart by: thinkorswim.com

Your goal is to retain the entire 8.7% and $400 credit by betting that the stock price will remain below the $100 price. It hasn't seen the $100 price point in over 12 months and getting up through that $100 will not be easy because it is considered a major level of resistance. The only thing that will move the stock up $10.50 from its current price is good news, so be sure you know when the company will be releasing their earnings.

After writing this section with Deere as an example for our bear call spread, the next day, the stock dropped $5.44 (Figure 9.4) dropping the credit of $1.00 to $.30 and an overnight gain of $700 based on 10 contracts. With this type of overnight profit I would defiantly set an order to close out the trade early and use the money for another trade because we still have two and a half weeks before the May expiration.

FIGURE 9.4   Stock Drops (DE)

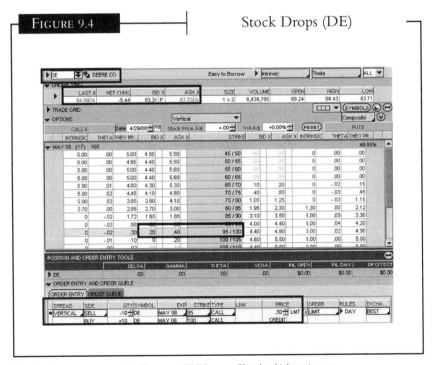

For color charts go to: www.traderslibrary.com/TLECorner • Chart by: thinkorswim.com

If you look at the bottom of Figure 9.5, you'll see that we have placed an order to close out the bear call vertical trade using a limit price of $.20; so, at any given time before the May expiration date if the spread reaches this price, our order will be executed. If this happens, we will have made $800, equaling a 19% return. If the order does not get filled at our limit price of $.20 and the stock remains below the $95 price, the order will expire worthless and will reach our maximum return of $1,000 or a 20% return.

Your first thought is probably to wait until expiration and collect the entire return; however, I would close out the trade, free up the money, and look for another opportunity because we still have two and a half weeks before expiration. Keep in mind that we're selling time (theta) so by finding another trade (even if it is a very conser-

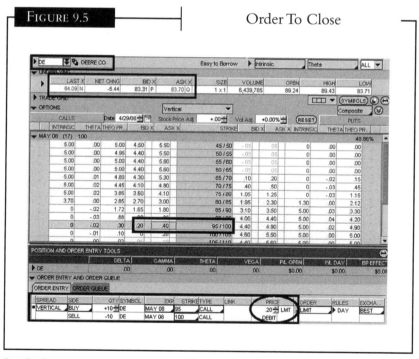

FIGURE 9.5 — Order To Close

For color charts go to: www.traderslibrary.com/TLECorner • Chart by: thinkorswim.com

190

vative trade), you'll still receive more than the $.20 or $.30 that's left on this trade.

KEEP LOOKING FOR PROFITABLE TRADES

Looking at Figures 9.6 and 9.7 you'll see why it is best to search for another trade. It took me about 10 minutes to find a bearish stock with a short-term resistance and a good premium for the next two and a half weeks. The stock is Martin Marietta Material (MLM), which is trading at $109.16 with a resistance at $115 and a major resistance level at $120, which is the 200-day moving average. Again, we're looking for stocks that show signs of weakness or that are in

FIGURE 9.6

Martin Marietta Material
Bear Call Spread

MLM Martin Marietta Material 109.16 -1.26 -1.14%

INERT(10,14,20) —45.49453 last=46.03161

For color charts go to: www.traderslibrary.com/TLECorner • Chart by: thinkorswim.com

a sideways trend. Then, we will select a price that we anticipate the stock will not move above come expiration date.

This example of MLM gave us a $.60 credit (or a $600 credit based on ten contracts) by selling the May $120 call option and buying the May $125 call option (Figure 9.7). Our goal was for the stock to remain below the $120 price, giving us a maximum profit of $600 and a rate of return of 13.6% for 2 ½ weeks.

Now, taking the previous trade on DE and this trade on MLM, your combined rate of return is 19% + 13.6% equaling 32.6% for 2 ½ weeks. I hope that I've encouraged you to not hold out for the last penny but to keep looking for other trades. The one thing I've learned about financial freedom is "your money must be working for you or you'll be working for your money." By the way, if ap-

FIGURE 9.7   Vertical Call Spread

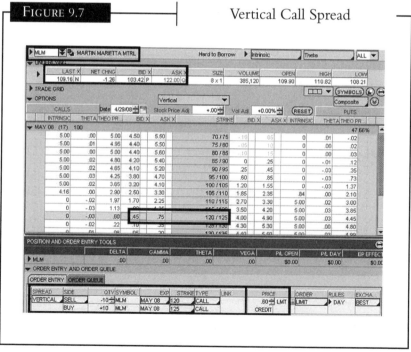

For color charts go to: www.traderslibrary.com/TLECorner • Chart by: thinkorswim.com

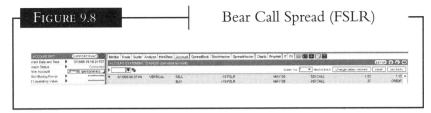

For color charts go to: www.traderslibrary.com/TLECorner • Chart by: thinkorswim.com

proved by your brokerage firm, these types of trades can be done within self-directed retirement accounts. Think about the power of getting 10 to 20% returns per month in a tax deferred account or think about earning 13% for 2 days.

Another bear call trade, Figure 9.8, is a two day trade, which I placed on Thursday the 15th, the Friday before the May expiration. The

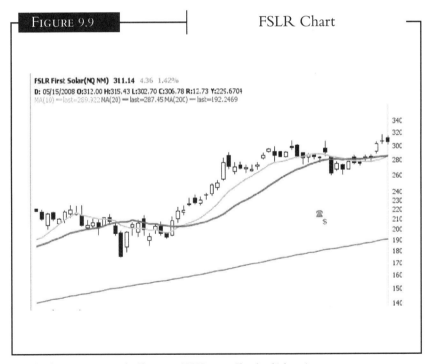

For color charts go to: www.traderslibrary.com/TLECorner • Chart by: thinkorswim.com

goal was for the stock FSLR to remain below the upper strike price of $320, and then I'd keep the entire $1,150 credit. As you'll see in the chart (Figure 9.9), FSLR closed at $311.14, so I allowed the trade to expire worthless without having to even pay a commission.

All of these strategies have one common goal: they will make your money work for you! This essentially means a more secure retirement and future for you and your family.

This is another example of selling an option instead of buying an option, which allows theta to melt away. I will only place credit spreads one to two weeks before the current expiration if the theta (time decay) of the selected vertical spread is high (and in this example the theta was $.54 per day). As we close out this chapter, it's important for you to understand that perfection comes from practice. The best practice you'll ever have will be with real money, but you must begin with single contracts until you can perfect your skills. I'm a strong believer in technical indicators, which helps me enhance my skills and build my confidence. The use of multiple moving averages was a confirmation to me that the stock would not move much because the two moving averages flattened out.

Self-test questions

1. In a bear call vertical spread, the lower strike price is the option that you'll what?

   A. Buy
   B. Sell

2. Your ultimate goal when placing a vertical call spread is for the price of the stock to move where?

   A. Higher
   B. Lower
   C. Sideways
   D. Any of the above as long as the stock price remains below the strike price

3. The ideal time to place a vertical bear call spread is?

   A. One month before expiration
   B. Two months before expiration
   C. Three months before expiration

4. When placing a vertical call spread, you need to determine the stock's what?

   A. Current trend
   B. Support Level
   C. Resistance Level

5. If you're looking to place more of a conservative call spread, you'd want to choose which of the following strike prices?

    A. Closest to the current price of the stock

    B. Above the current price of the stock

    C. Below the current price of the stock

6. If you placed a 10 contract vertical spread and sold the $100 strike price and purchased the $105 strike price for a credit of $1.10, what could be your maximum loss?

    A. $5,000

    B. Unlimited

    C. $3,900

7. If you were to close out your trade early for any reason, which strike price would be more important to close?

    A. The lower leg, which is the one you sold

    B. The upper leg, which is the one you bought

    C. Either the upper or lower; it doesn't matter

8. True or False: You can place vertical spread trades in a self-directed retirement account?

    A. True

    B. False

9. In addition to the use of the stock's resistance level, vertical call traders should also use what?

    A. Moving Averages

    B. MACD

    C. Stochastics

10. If the price of the stock closes in between your two strike prices, your loss would be?

    A. Maximum loss, which is the difference between your two strike prices

    B. Just the amount equal to the credit you received

    C. Difference between the two strike prices minus the credit received

For answers, go to www.traderslibrary.com/TLEcorner.

Ten

Taking Flight with Iron Condors

IN THIS CHAPTER

Russell 2000 example iron condor trade
Understanding "legging in"
Putting it all together- why this is a great conservative strategy

AN IRON CONDOR IS no more than two option spreads put together; to be more precise it's a bear call spread and a bull put spread placed on the same stock, ETF, or index for the same expiration month. An iron condor aims for the ultimate goal, which is for the investment of choice to remain below the lower leg of the bear call spread and above the upper leg of the bull put spread.

What if I was to say that if done correctly and following all the rules and the various do and don'ts of placing iron condors, you could consistently generate, on average, about 5 to 15% return per month? That's right; I said 5 to 15% per month.

A LOOK AT THE RUSSELL 2000

I'll take an example of the Russell 2000 index and walk you through the entry point and exit points and then share with you the results of this example along with the rate of return for the month. As with any trade, especially an option trade, you need to begin with the

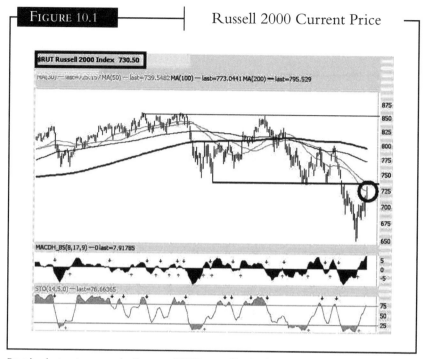

FIGURE 10.1 Russell 2000 Current Price

For color charts go to: www.traderslibrary.com/TLECorner • Chart by: thinkorswim.com

chart and determine the price high and low for the past one year and then the support and resistance level for the past one year. Using the Russell 2000 index as our first example, you'll see in Figure 10.1 that the Russell 2000 is currently at a price of 730. At the time we enter the iron condor trade the one year price high is 850 and the one year low is 650.

ESTABLISH SUPPORT AND RESISTANCE LEVELS

Identifying the 12-month support and resistance levels are important. These numbers make a huge difference in determining which strike prices to choose and will help you time your entry and even

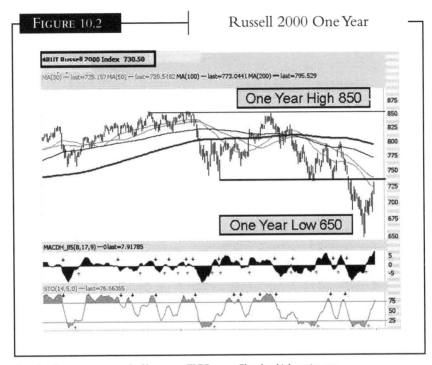

FIGURE 10.2 | Russell 2000 One Year

For color charts go to: www.traderslibrary.com/TLECorner • Chart by: thinkorswim.com

more important help you to exit early if the Russell 2000 reaches either the high of 850 or the low of 650. Figure 10.2 shows the 12-month price high of 850 and the 12-month low of 650, which can be referred to as the longer-term resistance (850) and long-term support (650).

Now that we have established the longer-term support and resistance levels, we will look at the short-term support and resistance levels to make sure we select strike prices that are high enough above resistance and low enough below support (Figures 10.3 and 10.4).

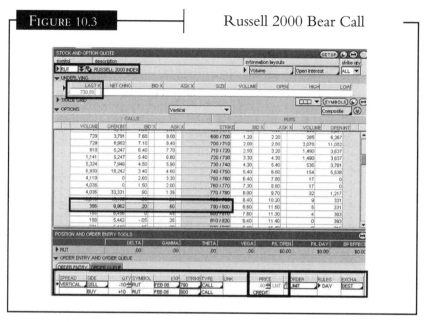

For color charts go to: www.traderslibrary.com/TLECorner • Chart by: thinkorswim.com

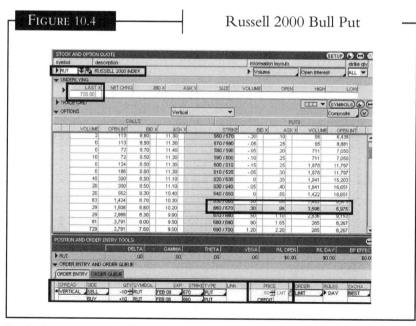

For color charts go to: www.traderslibrary.com/TLECorner • Chart by: thinkorswim.com

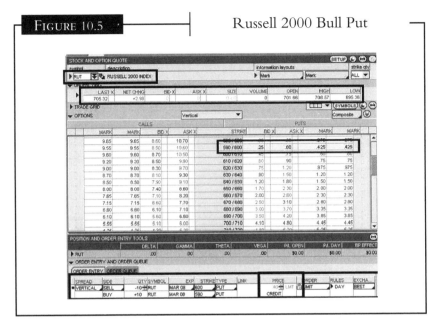

FIGURE 10.5 · | Russell 2000 Bull Put

For color charts go to: www.traderslibrary.com/TLECorner • Chart by: thinkorswim.com

SPLIT THE TRADE

Our second example of the Russell 2000 is for the following month (March) except we're going to split the trade and show you the price of the bull put spread for both the day we entered the trade and the price five weeks later, on expiration date. Looking at Figure 10.5, first you'll notice that we selected the 600/590 put spread when the Russell 2000 was trading at $705.32 and our credit was $.40 per share; so, based on a 10 contract trade, our credit is $400 for the five week trade. Our goal for the bottom leg put spread (upper leg is the bear call spread) will be for the Russell 2000 to remain above our chosen price of 600 come March expiration.

Our second example of this trade (Figure 10.6) shows a zero balance for the 600/590 put spread on the March expiration when the Russell 2000 is at 664, giving us the perfect situation for this trade. Our goal was to have the Russell 2000 remain above our 600 price,

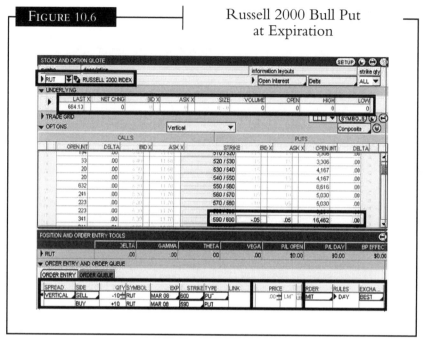

FIGURE 10.6 — Russell 2000 Bull Put at Expiration

For color charts go to: www.traderslibrary.com/TLECorner • Chart by: thinkorswim.com

which allows the time premium (theta) to erode away so we keep the $400 for a 4% return. Now keep in mind that an iron condor has two spread trades, a bull put spread and a bear call spread, so this rate of return is based solely on the put spread premium alone.

Let's now review Figure 10.7, which is the upper leg of the spread (bear call spread). By selecting the March 800/810 spread (Figure 10.8) when the Russell 2000 was trading at 705, we were able to collect a credit of $.20 per share, giving us $200 for 10 contracts. Our goal was to have the Rus-

REVIEW

An iron condor trade is made up of two spread trades. Keep this in mind when you are calculating your total rate of return. You need to calculate the bull put then the bear call and then combine them for your total.

FIGURE 10.7 — Russell 2000 Bear Call

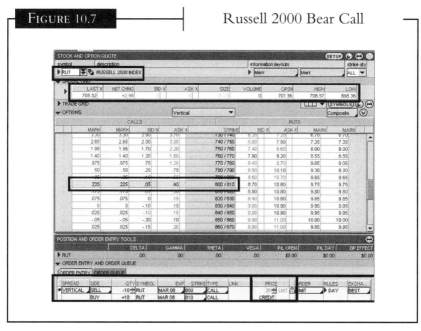

For color charts go to: www.traderslibrary.com/TLECorner • Chart by: thinkorswim.com

FIGURE 10.8 — Russell 2000 Bear Call at Expiration

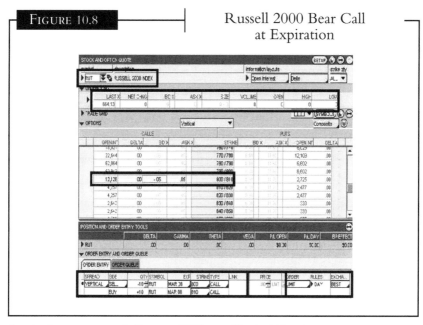

For color charts go to: www.traderslibrary.com/TLECorner • Chart by: thinkorswim.com

sell 2000 remain below the 800 strike allowing the spread to expire worthless and giving us a $200 profit for 10 contracts. Now, putting both this $200 profit with the $400 bull put profit, our total profit for five weeks is $600, equaling a rate of return of 6.4%. With the Russell 2000 closing at 664 on the third Friday of March, both the call and put spread expire worthless, allowing us to keep both the $.40 and $.20 premium and avoid any additional commissions.

Many of you are wondering how I came up with a 6.4% rate of return for five weeks (Figure 10.9). Let's walk through it together. You first total up your credits for the two trades ($600) then subtract the credit from $10,000, which is the difference between either your 800/810 bear call spread or the 600/590 bull put spread, leaving a cash requirement of $9,400. Last, we divide the $9,400 by the profit of $600 for a 6.4% rate of return.

Add profit from bear call and bull put: $200 + $400 = $600

Find the difference between your bear call spread and your bull put spread and your profit: $10,000 - $600 = $9,400 (cash requirement)

Divide the cash by the profit: $9,400/600 x 100 = 6.4%

Now, you must verify that your brokerage firm doesn't require $10,000 for each of the spreads (bull put and bear call). I say this because some brokerage firms will make that a requirement if you're going to place an iron condor even though it is impossible to lose on both trades; the closing price of the Russell 2000 cannot be above 800 and below 600 on expiration day. Although I don't agree, it is something to be aware of because it will require you to have an additional $10,000 and it would drop your rate of return to 3.1%.

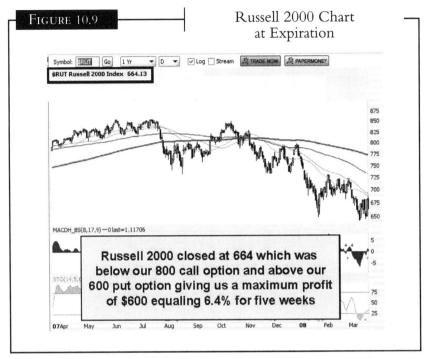

FIGURE 10.9 — Russell 2000 Chart at Expiration

Symbol: $RUT Go 1 Yr ▼ D ▼ ☑ Log ☐ Stream 🔒 TRADE NOW 🔒 PAPERMONEY

$RUT Russell 2000 Index 664.13

MACDH_BS(8,17,9) —0 last=1.11706

Russell 2000 closed at 664 which was below our 800 call option and above our 600 put option giving us a maximum profit of $600 equaling 6.4% for five weeks

STC(14.5,0

For color charts go to: www.traderslibrary.com/TLECorner • Chart by: thinkorswim.com

ADVANCED EXAMPLE

Because this is such a great strategy, I'm going to walk you through one more; but, this example is only for those of you that have larger sized accounts, have truly perfected this strategy, and know when and how to close out the trade if the stock market rallies dramatically up or falls dramatically down.

With 30 days before the May expiration, we're going to place a May 760/770 call spread and a May 620/610 put spread. This creates a credit of $1.60 per share, equaling $160 per contract. At the time of the trade, the Russell 2000 was trading at 689, which allows an

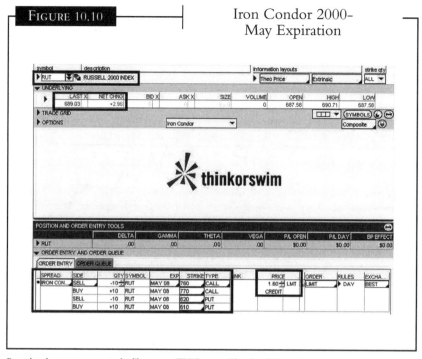

FIGURE 10.10 | Iron Condor 2000– May Expiration

For color charts go to: www.traderslibrary.com/TLECorner • Chart by: thinkorswim.com

upside cushion of 61 points and a downside cushion of 69 points with a maximum risk of $840 based on one contract (or $8,400 based on 10 contracts). Our rate of return if the Russell 2000 remains at any price between 760 and 620 is 19% for five weeks (see Figure 10.10).

To finalize this strategy you'll need to have a few guidelines to follow to both help increase your odds of success and also limit your risk. Legging into or out of the spread is acceptable and often a good way to put on the iron condor spread trade.

LEGGING IN

To leg into the trade, you'll place either the lower put trade or the upper leg call spread first, and then enter the other trade at another time. I prefer to enter the iron condor once my investment makes an obvious move in one direction or the other. For example, if I were to place an iron condor on the Russell 2000, I would enter the vertical put spread once the index has stopped a downward movement and a support level has been established.

This will do two things for you. First, it can increase your odds of being right. The belief is that because the Russell 2000 has established a support level, the odds of moving higher are greater. Second, it can increase the premium credit you'll receive because put option premiums increase when prices drop.

LINGO

"Legging in" is a trading strategy that involves placing one part of the spread trade before the other once the underlying security has made an obvious move in one direction or another.

This also works vice versa. I would leg into the upper call option vertical spread once the investment reached a level of resistance (ceiling). In this case, the Russell 2000 will need larger amounts of volume to break through resistance, and during the bullish upward movement, the price of call options are increasing, which will increase the credit amount you'll collect. If this strategy interests you, then you'll need to be good at evaluating an option's theta as well as the probability of expiring. Because an iron condor consists of selling two vertical spreads, theta will tell you how much time will erode over the life of the option and probability of expiring will give you the percentage of your option expiring within a certain strike price.

Let's review a chart of the Russell 2000 to help us place an iron condor for the month of June about six weeks before the June expiration. Looking at Figure 10.11 the first thing we see is the major resistance level of the 200-day moving average, which is at the $750 price. This helps us determine the upper legs of the iron condor

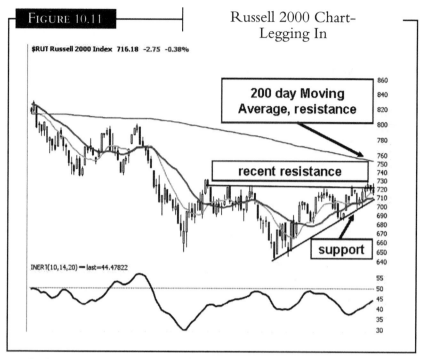

FIGURE 10.11 — Russell 2000 Chart– Legging In

$RUT Russell 2000 Index 716.18 -2.75 -0.38%

200 day Moving Average, resistance

recent resistance

support

INERT(10,14,20) — last=44.47822

For color charts go to: www.traderslibrary.com/TLECorner • Chart by: thinkorswim.com

because we know that with the Russell 2000 at 716, it's going to need a big boost of energy to move above this $750 price and stay above it. The next step is to identify the support level for the Russell 2000, which appears to be the 710 price range based on the short-term support and 640 being the longer-term support. Our goal is to now select a bear call and bull put spread based on the range of the Russell 2000.

Figure 10.12 shows an order entry to place the June iron condor giving you a $.80 credit for 6 weeks. We have chosen two very conservative spread trades while the Russell 2000 trades at $716. Our upper leg of the trade is an $810 and $820 bear call spread and the lower leg of our trade is the $620 and $610 bull put spread.

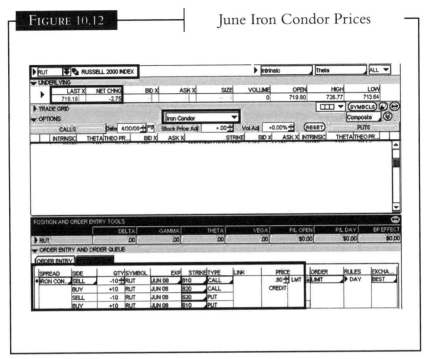

FIGURE 10.12 — June Iron Condor Prices

For color charts go to: www.traderslibrary.com/TLECorner • Chart by: thinkorswim.com

As you'll notice with these very conservative trades, we're allowing 94 points of upside cushion and 96 points of downside cushion. This means that the Russell 2000 can go up 94 points to $810 and we win. It can go down 96 points to $620 and we still win. Ideally, we need the Russell 2000 to close at any price between $810 and $620 and both sides of the iron condor will expire worthless, giving us an 8.7% rate of return.

Your rate of return is the same regardless if you're trading 1 contract or 100 contracts. Your credit is $80 per $920 of risk but even thought I use the word risk, I want you to understand that this is your maximum risk if the Russell 2000 closed above or below your chosen spread price. As you learn more about iron condors, you'll learn more about buying back and rolling out, which is closing both sides of the spread trade and selling the next month out or moving your strike prices higher or lower to avoid the risk of the Russell 2000 reaching your prices, respectively.

LINGO

Buying back is a risk/reward strategy that means investors choose to close out both sides of their spread trade in order to open a new trade for the next month.

Rolling out is a strategy that involves moving your strike prices out further in time in order to avoid the risk of your stock reaching them.

Once you allow the price to close above (lower strike price of the call option) or below (higher strike price of the put option) your spread price after the Thursday expiration (this index expires on the third Thursday of each month), no matter how high or low the Russell 2000 goes above or below your chosen strike prices, there cannot be any execution (purchase or sale) until after that third Thursday. If it does break up or down through those chosen strikes, you don't have to overreact and close the trade unless you believe it cannot stay within your spread range come expiration. As a word of caution I have been taught to close out the trades 4 to 10 days before the expiration date because the options market tends to see more movement during the last week of expiration, which increases your risk of the stock moving above or below your chosen strike prices and puts the trade in danger.

A Conservative Strategy with Huge Potential

Looking back at Figure 10.12, we're getting a $.80 credit, and we have close to a 100 point cushion on each side of the trades we placed. You can tighten up the strike price by choosing lower strike prices on the call options and higher strike prices on the put options; yet, you'll be increasing your risk.

This type of strategy is designed to be conservative while creating consistency; but, if your real money experience proves to pay off, then think about the opportunity of trading 50 or 100 contracts each month with $.80 credit per contact. It really adds up quickly ($.80 x 100 contracts = $8,000). Of course, if you're trading 100 contracts and receiving an $8,000 credit, you'll need to have $92,000 available within your trading account. Think about the type of return you would have if this was your perfected strategy of choice. You could generate about an 8% return every 6 weeks, and doing so in a self-directed retirement account would equal about 64% annually.

Self-test questions

1. An iron condor consists of how many different option trades?

    A. One

    B. Two

    C. Three

2. An iron condor can be placed on which of the following type of investments?

    A. Individual stocks

    B. Indexes

    C. Exchange Traded Funds

    D. All of the Above

3. True or False: It is important when placing an iron condor trade that you place both the call and put option trade at the same time.

    A. True

    B. False

4. Regardless of your profit, it is best to close out your trade _____ days before the expiration date.

    A. Two

    B. Three

    C. Four to seven days

5. If you were to place an iron condor buying and selling the calls and the puts each with a $10 spread for 10 contracts and a credit of $1.50, what would be your margin requirement?

   A. Ten thousand dollars
   B. Eighty-five hundred dollars
   C. Twenty thousand dollars

6. Assuming you have your iron condor trade in place and the price of the underlying security moves above the upper prices of the call spread, what do you do?

   A. Nothing until the week of expiration
   B. Close out just the upper call spread
   C. Close out both sides of the trade and take your loss

7. When placing an iron condor on an index, stock, or Exchange Traded Fund, you're looking for strike prices that are?

   A. In-the-money
   B. At-the-money
   C. Out-of-the-money

8. True or False: Besides knowing your risks, when placing an iron condor you must also know your costs.

   A. True
   B. False

9. If you are in an iron condor trade and the stock begins moving up, which leg of the spread should you close if you want to be profitable and limit your risk?

    A. The upper legs (call spread)

    B. The bottom legs (put spread)

    C. Just the upper leg of the bottom spread (put spread)

10. Before entering your trade you'll need to first determine the stock's?

    A. Support level and resistance level

    B. P/E ratio

    C. Current trend

For answers, go to www.traderslibrary.com/TLEcorner.

Conclusion

TRULY, IT'S NOT THE conclusion; it's only the beginning of an incredible investment journey, like the one I took over 10 years ago.

My goal for this book was to introduce you to a few of the most popular types of option strategies and various technical indicators that can increase your rates of return while limiting your risk. Thinking back to the introduction, I'd like to remind you that the most important key to financial freedom is the rate of return. May I encourage you to step outside of your comfort level and study the various ways you can increase your rate of return with the use of options.

Within these 10 chapters I outlined various ways to make money in the stock market using an aggressive "get rich" account to increase the rate of return using the leverage of call options or put options for both bullish and bearish markets. As you read further, we outlined covered call options, a great investment strategy for stock owners who are looking to benefit during up or sideway markets. If you remember, covered call options involve selling an option against the stock you own to generate monthly income. Keep in mind that the strike price you sell will determine the odds of you having to sell the stock; so, if you're really bullish on the stock, sell the higher strike price. If you're neutral to bearish on the stock's direction, sell the strike price that is closest to the current price of the stock; this will increase your odds of having to sell the stock while also increasing your premium.

If you were excited about the covered call chapter, then I'm sure you found a lot of value in the spread trade chapters, which are similar to covered calls except you don't have to own the stock. With spread trades you could be wrong about the direction of the stock and still be profitable.

But my favorite—our first chapter on technical indicators, because without them, I know I wouldn't be as successful. Just take the VIX indicator; if you didn't know when the market was at greatest risk to go down, you could stand to lose a lot of money. And, if you couldn't time the bullish run, you wouldn't make as much money.

Instead of searching for words, I'm going to close by thanking you for your support as well as for the purchase of this book. A portion of the book proceeds will be donated to the Alzheimer's Foundation.

As a final thought, please remember that most people spend more money on an automobile than their financial education; please do not be one of them! Learn how to properly manage your stock market investments because no one cares more about your money than you (or your kids). I look forward to meeting you some day at a live workshop. I ask that you keep your eyes and ears open for my next educational release (mid to late 2009), which will be an educational stock market board game—educational and fun for the entire family. Thank you and happy trading!

Appendix A

Advanced Order Feature on thinkorswim.com

FIGURE A.1 SHOWS THE stock Visa trading at $83.23 per share. With the use of thinkorswim's advanced order feature, I can place an order to buy the July $80 call option at a limit price of $7.60. Once filled, I can trigger an advanced order to sell the option at the bid if the price of the stock drops to $80 per share or below. This is a powerful thinkorswim tool because as you get better at using technical indicators, you'll be entering and exiting your trades based on the information these technical indicators tell you.

If you know that when stocks break below their support level they move lower and if the support level for Visa was $80 per share, then you could sell your call option for the current bid price at the time the stock breaks below support. Please keep in mind that as the stock increases in value you'll want to increase the trigger price (sell price). Say that you purchase the call option at $7.60 when the stock was trading at $83.23. Then the stock moved up to $90 per share, increasing your option to $13.20.

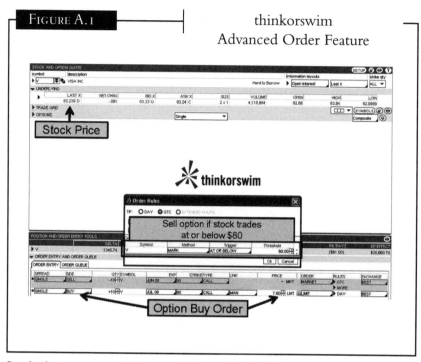

You'll want to change the trigger price of the stock from $80 per share to say, $87 per share, which will assure you that if the stock drops to $87 or lower, your advanced sell order is now selling the option at its current bid price. I know I've gone a little deeper into this and it is still a bit confusing, so the best thing for you to do is pick up the phone and call your broker of choice, and have them walk you through the order process.

Appendix B

Protect Your Assets

ASSET PROTECTION FOR INVESTORS

One of the most common questions an investors asks, do you run your trading like a business? And my answer is yes I do, however, I can't give you any legal advice as to which entity is best or why, as you'll need to consult your financial advisor or attorney. I can say this; that having a corporate brokerage account can have its advantages because more and more people are becoming concerned about asset protection and with very good reason. With lawyers being admitted to the bar in record numbers; local, state and federal taxes threatening to take more and more of our hard-earned income; and with the population becoming more and more lawsuit happy, those of us with assets want to keep them. It doesn't matter how you acquired your assets. The important thing is that you want to keep them! You don't want to give them to every person, government, or "good cause" that comes knocking on your door with their hand out. You want to provide for your own family and retirement because there is little doubt that those of us who have not yet started to collect Social Security payments will never see a fair return on the money we have paid into the system. You also want to provide for your children or grandchildren so they may not have to struggle quite as long and hard as you did during your life. And finally, there is the thought that "Darn it! I earned this money. I want to spend it according to my needs and not those of the government, or the courts."

THE ASSET PROTECTION ENTITIES

If you are an investor, how do you protect your stock trading account? What entity, or entities, shall you use to protect these assets so that you and your family receive the benefits of this account, and not the others that are always looking for ways to take your assets from you? There are several legal entities that you may use to protect your assets. Some of these are the C Corporation, a Limited Partnership (LP), and/or a Limited Liability Company (LLC). If you talk to 10 asset protection experts, you will probably receive about 12 different answers. But, which one is the best? And, more importantly, which is the best way for you to protect your assets? Not being an expert in this field or licensed to give advice on this subject I have to defer this to someone who can through their website www.cssnevada.com or by phone at 702-933-4030. When contacting CSS NEVADA, if you refer to the reference number EBM-08, they will honor a $100 discount towards services as a buyer of this book.

To read more, please visit: www.traderslibrary.com/TLEcorner

Glossary

Assignment: the process by which an option is exercised, with the obligation to buy shares under a call or to sell shares under a put.

At-the-money: the status of an option when the current price of the underlying stock is identical to the strike price.

Average True Range (ATR): the greatest of the absolute value of the current high less the previous close; or the absolute value of the current low less the previous close. ATR is a formula used to determine an appropriate price to avoid selling too soon or too late.

Beta: a measurement of a stock's price change in comparison to the broader market trend.

Bollinger Bands: a plotted band two standard deviations away from a simple moving average, which tends to widen as a stock's price becomes more volatile.

Buy back: closing out a position in order to initiate a new one.

Call: an option granting its owner the right, but not the obligation, to buy 100 shares of the underlying stock at the strike price on or before expiration.

Class: a distinction of all options for the same stock.

Closing transaction: an order that cancels an open position; a sell against a long position or a buy against a short position.

Combination: an option strategy with both calls and puts that is not a straddle.

Covered call: a short call entered when the trader also owns 100 shares of the underlying stock for each call written.

Delivery: satisfaction of the obligation under an option contract, consisting of the purchase of shares under terms of a call or the sale of shares under terms of a put.

Delta: a comparison between the degree of an option's price change and the price change of the underlying security.

Diagonal spread: a spread with options of different strike and expiration.

Early exercise: the exercise of an option before its expiration date.

Earnings per share (EPS): corporate earnings expressed on a per-share basis. Net earnings are divided by the average outstanding shares during the year, with the result expressed in dollars and cents.

Ease of movement: a momentum indicator tracking the relationship between price change and trading volume.

Equivalent position: a position using options that is the equivalent of a stock position, also called a synthetic position.

Expiration: the day on which an option becomes worthless or, if in-the-money, is exercised by its owner or by the exchange.

Extrinsic value: also called time value, that portion of an option premium excluding intrinsic value. Extrinsic value also includes volatility value, or the variable based on the volatility of the underlying stock.

Fibonacci ratios: a mathematical sequence of numbers in which each number is equal to the sum of the two previous numbers: 1,2,3,5,8,13,21, 34, 55. This sequencing is used by technicians to help determine retracements.

Gamma: a measurement of change in an option's delta per one-point change in the underlying stock.

Greeks: a series of value calculations named after letters of the Greek alphabet.

Horizontal spread: a spread with options of the same strike but different expirations.

Implied volatility: a prediction of the underlying stock's volatility based on trends in option values rather than on historical data of the stock.

In-the-money: the status of an option when the current price of the underlying stock is higher than a call's strike price, or lower than a put's strike price.

Inertia indicator: a method for determining the strength or weakness of price movement, based on degrees of change away from a norm or median price level.

Intrinsic value: the number of points an option is in-the-money; intrinsic value tracks changes in the underlying stock on a point-for-point basis.

Iron condor: a strategy combining two spreads together; it includes a bull spread and a bear spread with a total of four different strikes.

LEAPS (Long-term Equity Anticipation Securities): long-term option contracts with life spans up to 30 months. In comparison, standard listed options last only eight or nine months at the most.

Legging: entry into or exit from a combined trade (spread or straddle) in increments rather than both sides at the same time.

MACD: moving average convergence divergence, a technical indicator that tracks the change between two moving averages based on price.

Moving average: a method of evening out a trend by adding together a field of prices and dividing the total by the number of prices in the field; it is called a *moving* average because with each new entry, the oldest value is dropped.

Naked options: short positions not hedged with other option or stock positions. A naked call has unlimited risk and a naked put has limited risk.

Opening transaction: an order that opens a position, either a buy (long) or a sell (short).

Option: a contract granting its owner the right to buy 100 shares (call) or to sell 100 shares (put) of a specific underlying security, at a fixed strike price and on or before a specific expiration date.

Out-of-the-money: the status of an option when the current price of the underlying stock is lower than a call's strike price, or higher than a put's strike price.

Premium: the cost of an option, expressed on a per-share basis even though the option controls 100 shares. As a result, premium value has to be converted to dollar values. For example, premium of 3.50 is equal to $350.

Put: an option granting its owner the right, but not the obligation, to sell 100 shares of the underlying stock at the strike price on or before expiration.

Ratio write: a variation of the covered call, in which more calls are sold than stock is held (for example, if a trader owns 200 shares and sells 3 calls, it creates a 3:2 covered write).

Resistance: the highest point in a stock's current trading range; the highest price buyers are willing to pay under current conditions.

Rolling out: closing one option position and replacing it with another, usually applied to short positions. Options are rolled forward by replacing them with a later-expiring option of the same strike. Short calls may be closed and replaced with a roll up to a later-expiring option with a higher strike. Short puts may be rolled forward and down, replacing them with later-expiring puts with lower strikes.

Series: all options for one underlying stock with the same strike and expiration.

Spread: opening of long and short options on the same stock, designed to mitigate potential losses on the short side, with limited profit potential.

Stochastic oscillator: a technical indicator comparing closing price to price range of a stock, as a means of quantifying momentum.

Straddle: opening of an equal number of call and put options with the same terms (strike and expiration).

Strike price: the fixed price at which an option can be exercised.

Support: the lowest point in a stock's current trading range; the lowest price sellers are willing to accept under current conditions.

Theta: a measurement of time decay in an option over a period of time.

Time value: the portion of option premium other than intrinsic value, derived solely from the amount of time remaining until expiration.

Underlying security: the stock or index on which an option is bought or sold, which cannot be changed or transferred.

Vertical spread: a spread with options of the same expiration but different strikes.

Volatility value: the degree to which the price of the underlying security fluctuates.

RECOMMENDED READING

The Complete Guide to Technical Indicators
By: Larson, Mark
Item #: 5197572

Traders have used the power of technical indicators to put significant gains in their account. Now you can easily carve through the hundreds of indicators and get right to the ones that make money most often and help you achieve success in trading. In this comprehensive guide to cracking the code of technical indicators, best-selling author and acclaimed presenter, Mark Larson, shows you how to find the indicators that best fit your trading style and reveals which indicators work in which markets. With this experience, you will have the power to increase your winning percentage, no matter what the market does.

Option Volatility Trading Strategies
By: Natenberg, Sheldon
Item #: 5127729

Options traders make money any time the market moves, no matter whether it goes up or down. Since the inception of options only a few decades ago, many have sought to harness the key element of options trading—volatility. No one is more synonymous with volatility trading strategies than Sheldon Natenberg. Renowned for his influence on nearly every option trader through his classic work, Option Volatility and Pricing, this legend in trading success is in great demand for his ability to harness market forces through his calculated approach to trading. Now, in a groundbreaking new approach, Natenberg personally guides you through the key elements of option valuation and volatility trading strategies.

Option Spreads Made Easy Course Book with DVD
By: Fontanills, George
Item #: 5446423

George Fontanills, popular author of Trade Options Online and The Options Course and founder of Optionetics.com, hands you his proven techniques for profiting with option spreads. Included in this course book is a vivid 90-minute DVD and online access to charts and self exams to ensure that you digest all aspects of his winning techniques.

Fontanills shows you how you can use option spreads to expand your profit opportunities while managing your risk. With this ground-breaking DVD and book combination, you can pour over every word of Fontanills' presentation—learning each important point in a step-by-step, layer-by-layer process. Fontanills begins with a discussion on equity options and basic bull call spreads and continues with lessons on how to structure debit and credit spreads, what market conditions are most profitable, and how to achieve your trading goals by adjusting strike-price levels.

▲ ▲ ▲ ▲ ▲ ▲ ▲

To get the current lowest price on any item listed
Go to www.traderslibrary.com

B

Marketplace **Books** is the preeminent publisher of trading, investing, and finance educational material. We produce professional books, DVDs, courses, and electronic books (ebooks) that showcase the exceptional talent working in the investment world today. Started in 1993, Marketplace Books grew out of the realization that mainstream publishers were not meeting the demand of the trading and investment community. Capitalizing on the access we had through our distribution partner Traders' Library, Marketplace Books was launched, and today publishes the top authors in the industry—household names like Jack Schwager, Oliver Velez, Larry McMillan, Sheldon Natenberg, Jim Bittman, Martin Pring, and Jeff Cooper are just the beginning. We are actively acquiring some of the brightest new minds in the industry including technician Jeff Greenblatt and programmers Jean Folger and Lee Leibfarth.

From the beginning student to the professional trader, our goal is to continually provide the highest quality resources for those who want an active role in the world of finance. Our products focus on strategic information and cutting edge research to give our readers the best education possible. We are at the forefront of digital publishing and are actively pursuing innovative ways to deliver content. At our annual Traders' Forum event, our readers get the chance to learn and mingle with our top authors in a way unprecedented in the industry. Our titles have been translated in most major world languages and can be shipped all over the globe thanks to our preferred online bookstore, TradersLibrary.com.

VISIT US TODAY AT:

WWW.MARKETPLACEBOOKS.COM & WWW.TRADERSLIBRARY.COM